E-Mail From Nigeria

Also by Todd Allen

Beware the Club Girls

Todd Allen's work can also be found at
http://www.indignantonline.com

E-Mail From Nigeria

Todd Allen

Copyright ©2004 Todd Allen

ISBN #: 0-9749598-0-4
All rights reserved. No part of this book may be reproduced or transmitted in any form or by any means, electronic or mechanical, including photocopying, recording or by any information storage and retrieval system, without permission in writing form the copyright owner.

For more information, visit the website at www.indignantonline.com

This is a work of fiction. Names, characters, place and incidents either are the product of the author's imagination or are used fictitiously, and any resemblance to any actual persons, living or dead, events, or locales is entirely coincidental.

This book was printed in the United States of America

For anyone who thinks Michel Foucault just couldn't get over being unpopular as a child.

Index

Business, Political And Computer Problems

- E-Mail From Nigeria — p. 11
- Note to Telemarketers: This Is A Voice Mail — p. 14
- President Bush Seeks Consensus on Faith-Based Community Service From Clinton, Sharpton and Microsoft — p. 17
- Internet Typo Sparks Stock Rally — p. 20
- The Indignant Guide To MBA Admissions Essays — p. 22
- Donald Trump Will Steal Our Women — p. 26
- The Apartment Credit Check of Doom — p. 28
- Layoffs Hit Another Service Sector: Crystal Consulting — p. 32
- Avoiding The Ex-Boss, An Exercise In Espionage — p. 34
- Terror Grips McCormick As Local Publisher Tries To Drive — p. 39
- Enron: The Circle-Jerk of Backstabbing — p. 41
- Aerobics for a 5-Year-Old? Marketing to Crazed, Over-Weight Suburbanites — p. 44
- Secret Internet Crushes: Romance Or Trouble Coming Looking For You? — p. 47
- If The Political Parties Hate Each Other So Much, Give Congress An Open-Mike Night — p. 50

Women And Drinking

- Lingerie Shopping — p. 55
- Losing A Girl To Your Clone — p. 59
- Call Her Within Five Business Days Or I Take Her Number Back — p. 62
- Another Tale Of Money-Hungry Lincoln Park Girls — p. 64
- My Tourist Buddy And His Failed Fling — p. 67
- Her Gift In His Lap - A Comedy of Upset Stomachs — p. 72

- The Adventure Of The Sympathetic Waitress — p. 75
- Propositioned - In Front of Her Brothers — p. 78
- Behind The Orange Curtain
  OR
  The Naïve And Sentimental Patron — p. 81
- Hate Mail From A Spring Break College Girl Gone Wild — p.84
- The Virgin of Evanston Affair — p. 87
- An Over-Stimulated Drunk Woman Broke My Glasses — p. 92
- My New Definition Of A Hook-Up Bar — p. 94
- The Adventure Of The Middle-Aged Make-Out Table — p. 97

Travel

- Trapped In Flight Delay Hell — p. 103
- Breaking Down Racial Stereotypes... With A Radiation Suit — p. 110
- Beset By Hicks:
  My Sad Trip To The Alamo Bowl — p. 115

Pop Culture

- Something Else To Mix With Your Vodka — p. 125
- The Drowned Out Drummer, Another Insipid Nightclub Fad? — p. 127
- Oprah To Give United Nations A Spirit Makeover — p. 129
- Giants At The Movie Theater — p. 131
- Super Models Suppressing Puberty with Performance Enhancing Drugs — p. 134
- Hannibal Lauded For Positive Portrayal Of Cannibalism — p. 137

Just Plain Strange

- The Large Condom Phone Call — p. 141
- ... And Then They Stole His Shoes — p. 144

- Porn Bag or Comic Bag? p. 149
- Plushies – Fetishists Get It On With Stuffed Animals p. 152
- A Gift Registry For A Birthday Party p. 155
- It's All Good – A Slogan For Losers p. 158
- Beggars On The Bridge p. 161
- Suburbanites Don't Know Drums p. 164
- Understanding What the Policeman Says p. 167
- Fluffy Toilet Seat Covers p. 170
- The Migratory Effects Of The Smoking Ban p. 173

Business, Political And Computer Problems

E-Mail From Nigeria

Sometimes it amazes me how important certain people in Africa seem to think I am. Seems like at least twice a week I get an e-mail from Africa, usually from Nigeria, requesting my help with a sticky financial situation, which is kinda funny when you consider the size of the college loans I've still got. And I'm not just getting mail from your run of the mill Joe, either. No, it's the crème de la crème of society functions that are contacting me:

- "Dr. Patrick Omo," who identifies himself as a "Credit Officer with the Union Bank of Nigeria Plc, Lagos," and comes to me with a special business offer.
- "ALBERT OKUMAGBA," whose computer seemingly only types in capital letters, who claims to be "THE CHAIRMAN TENDER BOARD OF INDEPENDENT NATIONAL ELECTORAL COMMISSION (INEC)." Albert would like me to help him with a "TRANSFER OF FUND VALUED AT (US$21.6M) TO A SAFE FOREIGN ACCOUNT."
- "Mrs. Sese-seko widow of late President Mobutu Sese-seko of Zaire, now known as Democratic Republic of Congo (DRC)." She'd like my help in acquiring some of her late husband's frozen assets.
- "Mr. T. Savimbi, son of the late rebel leader, Jonas Savimbi of Angola who was killed on the 22nd of February 2002," has a similar tale to "Mrs. Sese-seko."
- "Nzanga JOSEPH (DÉSIRÉ) MOBUTU" says he's "the first son of the late JOSEPH (DÉSIRÉ) MOBUTU, the former President of the ZAIRE now democratic republic of congo." He's claiming to be in Nigeria and having similar problems to Mr. Savimbi and Mrs. Sese-seko.
- "Anderson K. Eseimoku" claims to be "a highly placed official of Government of Nigeria and also a

founding member of the ruling party in Power now, the Peoples Democratic Party(PDP)." He'd like me to help him lay hands on some oil money.

Golly gee whiz, isn't amazing how all these important people need my help? But then again, I'm betting this doesn't sound too unfamiliar to you. And could there be any other reason for so many people to be getting the same "confidential correspondence," than a scam in the offing? Of course not.

If you get a lot of these letters, you'll notice most of them are somehow connected to Nigeria, which is why this sort of e-mail is often referred to as either "The Nigerian Scam" or the "4-1-9 Scam," named after section 4-1-9 of the Nigerian criminal code that this sort of fraud falls under. It's widespread enough that www.fraudaid.com offers a comparison chart of various Nigerian Scam Letters, and even venerable Scotland Yard has a series of web pages on the topic (http://www.met.police.uk/fraudalert/419how.htm), going so far as to suggest that government officials may be involved with some of the scams.

The real fun part of the Nigerian scam comes when you're boneheaded enough to show up in Nigeria looking for your money. A college roommate of mine from Peru reports he had such a boneheaded friend, who almost got killed doing just that.

Amazing what you find in your e-mails these days.

But should you think that the Nigerian underworld is limiting themselves to spamming your mailbox, you'd be taking too dim a view of their sophistication. As I was writing this column, I was startled to see my publisher had processed an order for 25 copies of my book to be shipped to Lagos Island, Nigeria. Lagos is the former capital of Nigeria and widely believed to be the birthplace of the Nigerian Scam. Thinking this was a strange coincidence, I contacted my publisher and, sure enough,

E-Mail From Nigeria

those sneaky Nigerian cyber-gangsters credit card frauded my publisher out of those books, and have been hitting the publisher's website for the past few weeks.

Never let it be said that the Nigerian scam-artists will let a little detail like learning new technologies stand between them and a con. And I suppose I should be flattered I'm considered worth stealing. In the record industry, that's high praise.

Still, it's probably best to keep one hand on your e-wallet when the Nigerians start e-mailing you. And G.W.? As long as you've got some troops in the neighborhood, I wouldn't mind getting my books back. Stolen American property and all...

Todd Allen

Note To Telemarketers: This Is A Voice Mail

Telemarketers. Does anyone not hate telemarketers? There's only one thing worse than telemarketers, and that's the really dumb ones that can't tell the difference between live and voicemail.

No, I'm serious.

For the past week, I've been getting one or two messages per day from some dipstick who sounds very much like a telemarketer. There's no number associated with the incoming call, which usually means a blocked-number telemarketing firm. The message always consists of an opening along the lines of the "hey, how you doing" method of the telemarketer trying to establish rapport with the victim before letting them know who's talking to them. And it's the same voice. You'd think, just maybe, this genius would figure out he was talking to voice mail.

And, to make it worse, this grand invader of my privacy has a bad habit of calling about half an hour before I'm planning on getting out of bed. There's nothing quite as aggravating as groggily pulling yourself out of bed and hearing "hey amigo," from some overly-perky salesman who can't even bother to say what he wanted before hanging up.

There are of course, worse things than sales cold calls. I have had the unusual experience of moving into an apartment that kept the same phone number as the previous tenant. It has, for the most part, subsided, but when I moved in, I used to get a fair amount of calls for the previous resident that sounded an awful lot like collection agencies. They'd never say exactly what they wanted, but I had the worst time convincing some of the people that nobody by that name really lived here. I can think of more productive activities while I'm home.

What's the government doing about this, you might ask? Well, the Federal Trade Commission is trying to create a national "do not call" registry, where Joe Consumer can register their number and make it illegal for, Verizon, to use the example of one telemarketing call I put up with, this week, to call you, and it would be subject to fine. As of March 11, 2003, the bill allowing for appropriations for the construction of the Do Not registry was signed into law, so the FTC should start building the list anytime now. (For more information on this program, including when you can finally opt-out, consult the FTC website at: http://www.ftc.gov/bcp/conline/edcams/donotcall/index.html) It's likely that various Direct Marketing agencies will try to sue and block the Do Not Call registry, do if you should have occasion to bump into your Senator or Representative, it wouldn't hurt to tell them how happy you are about the FTC and avoiding telemarketers. Uh, oh... I just said something nice about the government. In the interest of popular opinion, I'd best switch topics.

As we wait for that wonderful directory to be built, all we can really do is tell the telemarketers to take our number off their list. Given the number of hang-ups and partial messages I've been getting, I've decided to take that path one step further.

My outgoing voice mail message now plays as follows:

"If this is yet another telemarketer who can't distinguish an outgoing message on a voice mail system from an actual person answering the phone, please delete this number immediately. However, if you're not a telemarketer, go ahead... leave a message."

Perhaps they're all using automated dialers and won't hear my greeting, or lack thereof. Perhaps they won't actually delete my number. But if that outgoing message gets my name off just one list without having to have my precious time wasted, then its well worth my time to put it there.

I encourage everyone else to do the same. Let's give those speed-dialing cretins a hint of how much business they're going to be out when the do not call directory gets built.

E-Mail From Nigeria

President Bush Seeks Consensus On Faith-Based Community Service From Clinton, Sharpton And Microsoft

(Washington, DC) President G.W. Bush has spent the last week vigorously promoting his new White House Office of Faith-Based and Community Initiatives and has received a multitude of offers from a bi-partisan assortment of groups.

"I've always encouraged consensus building," President Bush said in a prepared statement. "I think it's important we all get on the same page when dealing with the good of the country. Just as I gave credit to former President Clinton at my Notre Dame graduation speech, for reducing the number of welfare recipients, I'm equally glad Bill has agreed to join me in bi-partisan support of community actions."

While not going so far as to endorse the White House Office of Faith-Based and Community Initiatives, Bill Clinton did comment on the value of community-based social services.

"As my wife Hilary has said on occasion, it takes a village to raise a child." Clinton began. "Hilary and I have already raised one child, and since Hilary's spending so much time in Washington, I have more time on my hands to give back to the community. I am especially concerned that many of our young people are unaware of the dangers of unsafe sex. I welcome any help in educating young people in my new community, and I've never been one to discriminate by faith in such situations."

Also joining in with offers of help was the Reverend Al Sharpton, who has recently declared his intent to run for president on the Democratic ticket in 2004.

"I'm not willing to admit anyone has more experience talking to the people than I do," Sharpton told reporters. "As a reverend and as a community activist, I would be more than willing to extend my services to the White House. I'll handle all the communications for them. People love to hear from me. Besides, I need to get my foot in the door while Jesse Jackson's still keeping a low profile."

Just as the left wing is lining up to help out, so is the religious right. Former presidential candidate and evangelist, Pat Robertson is seeking to apply for matching funds for his healthcare initiatives. Robertson, though he has not done so in recent years, made practice of asking people to touch the television set and be healed through faith when he began broadcasting his 700 Club television program in the 1970s. Robertson is said to be contemplating a return to faith healing if he can receive one of Bush's "charitable choice" social service contracts.

Evangelist and faith healer, Benny Hinn is positioning himself from a different angle. Hinn seeks to receive a portion of the proposed $1.6 billion earmarked for drug treatment. Sources close to Hinn indicate Hinn sees very little difference between "breathing the breath of God" into a believer and restoring the ability to hear and "breathing the breath of God" into a believer and driving out a drug addiction. As such, Hinn figures he's in line for federal funding.

On the other hand, the White House Office of Faith-Based and Community Initiatives had to turn down education programs from Microsoft and Apple Computers. Upon investigating the proposed programs, the Office discovered that the computer vendors treat their products much like a religious faith. They further found that many computer professionals referred to Windows vs. Apple as a religious choice. Based on the religious aspects of their education plans, the Office was forced to turn them down. As president Bush said, "Government should never fund the teaching of faith, but it should support the good works of the faithful."

The White House Office of Faith-Based and Community Initiatives said it would be happy to work with Microsoft or Apple on more secular projects, like assisting with Habitat For Humanity or feeding the homeless.

Todd Allen

Internet Typo Sparks Stock Rally

(NY, NY) A typo in a market forecast by on-line broker Roofus, Doofus & Co. has had Wall Street spinning and Human Genome stocks rising, from the oddest of places – fantasy role-playing gamers.

When Winston Twiddle, a senior analyst with Roofus, Doofus & Co., keyed in his report on the prospects of the biotech stock sector, he left an "e" out of genome and touted the upside of stocks tracking the genetic code of gnomes. While the average investor would be unlikely to see this as anything other than a typo, through the speed of the Internet, word of gnome investment opportunities spread quickly to realm of online gamers, who frequently encounter gnomes in games such as Dungeons & Dragons and War Hammer. Gnomes are a race of small, dwarf-like people traceable to Norse mythology and perhaps best known as the little statues in people's gardens.

The result was a newly tapped circle of individual investors pumping an estimated 34.7 million dollars into genome stocks like Celera and Human Genome Sciences, Inc., driving shares up an average of 28%.

"This may sound out of place," said Barry Milhorn, a stockbroker specializing in the portfolios of the socially phobic. "But the entire gnome typo has unearthed a new type of investor. An investor whose needs are not being served in the current climate. An investor I like to call the 'flexible reality' investor."

Milhorn credited the popularity of games like Magic: The Gathering and the long-awaited film version of the

E-Mail From Nigeria

Dungeons and Dragons game with creating a climate conducive to investment in gnomes. Milhorn said more typos of that nature would only be good for the market and it would be particularly good for his commissions if someone would write about a publicly traded company manufacturing Kryptonite.

Strangely enough, once word of the typo got out, while trading on genome stocks did slow down, the price did not dip back to pre-gnome levels, and the investors who got in on the fantasy-buying frenzy do not appear to have cashed in the stocks upon learning of the error.

"What, you want me to ruin their day," Milhorn seemed skeptical about an investor sell-off. "These guys paid good money to invest in the genetic sequencing of an imaginary life form and you want me to tell them they're wrong? It would kill them, and let's face it, anyone who'd invest in a company specializing in gnomes isn't too likely to be reading the newspaper everyday. It's best we leave them to their fantasies."

Todd Allen

The Indignant Guide To MBA Admissions Essays

Thinking about going back to school to get your MBA? Can't figure out what the university wants out of that admissions essay where you're supposed describe how your life experience has been leading you towards your MBA and what you plan do with your life after you get it? Not sure how to fake the entrepreneurial inclinations the B-schools crave in applicants? Afraid to admit the only reason you want an MBA is to impress chicks? Fear no more, Indignant Online has found the Harvard MBA admission essay by Joey Loser, a corporate toady, just like you. Follow Joey's structure and his single-minded candor, and we're sure you'll get into Harvard, too.

Please Let Me Into Harvard Business School

By

Joey Loser, Corporate Toady

Please let me into Harvard Business School. I have spent my entire life in the pursuit of cheap beer and agreeable women while developing an entrepreneurial spirit in a consulting vein. The only thing that stands between myself and the intimate company of socially acceptable women is the respect that a piece of paper declaring me a graduate of your fine program brings.

I came from a small town and a humble background. I was a very ugly child. The girls would not have sex with me because I was very ugly. Becoming frustrated, I tried the boys, but they would not have sex with me either, because I had horrible acne on my bottom. I tried sheep, but I was not very athletic and the sheep would run away from me. So I grew up very frustrated.

Eventually, my parents sent me to college. As I was not very bright, they could not send me to a good school like the University of Chicago, where I could meet women in an environment where all the men were as geeky as myself. I was only able to go to Deewllid University, where the men were all better looking than me and hoarded all the women. It was all right, though because there were high school girls near the campus, and they were easily impressed by the fact I was in college, so I was able to have sex for the first time.

It was good.

Then I graduated from college. When I was no longer in school and didn't have a job, the high school girls' parents realized what was going on and ran me out of town. I moved to New York and got a job in the mailroom at a Wall Street firm. I tried dating but all the brokers hogged all the women. Then I discovered how easy the students at NYU are. They were easily impressed that I had a job and I was able to have sex again.

It was good.

Eventually, I was able to convince a management-consulting firm in Cleveland that my time in the mailroom made me an expert on corporate structure and information flow. That firm offered me more money to move to Cleveland. Since everything is cheaper in Cleveland, including prostitutes, I discovered I could have even more sex and a larger apartment, so I moved. Consulting seemed to be a perfect match for a man of my ambitions. I dutifully studied the film, "In the Company of Men," and it helped me greatly in my duties.

Todd Allen

It was good.

Until I realized that I couldn't afford my large apartment and my prostitutes when combined with the massive medical bills from all the diseases I caught from my prostitutes. Especially when the firm wouldn't let me use my expense account for the prostitutes.

So I moved back to New York. Unfortunately, as easy as they are, the NYU girls are terrible lays compared to Cleveland whores. Fortunately, my new company in New York is a dot com consultancy, and while they don't let me have an expense account, I was able to share my knowledge of expense accounts with my new clients, thus increasing everyone's enjoyment, and developing my entrepreneurial spirit as I developed expense account work-arounds for all parties involved. And there are plenty of gold diggers at industry events, so I could have sex again.

It was good.

Unfortunately, the gold diggers are always trying to get knocked up, and condoms are expensive and cutting into my spending money. I also have to pretend I have stock options and I keep slipping up.

All my life I've been upgrading the quality of my sex, from high school girls to college girls to prostitutes to gold diggers. I realize that I need to take the next step. I need to have sex with women who can afford their own birth control, so I afford to buy the more risqué foreign editions of Playboy with my disposable income. Unfortunately, I am a lowly Internet executive from a small town. Socially acceptable women will not talk to me, for I have not yet achieved the proper pedigree. Were socially acceptable women, that happened to be rich, ever to talk to me, and if the sex was good enough, I might even contemplate marriage as I am approaching middle age and it might help with promotions.

E-Mail From Nigeria

In order to have sex with socially acceptable women, I must improve myself, or at least be able to show them a piece of paper that says I improved myself. I figured I would need to either get a law degree or an MBA. I figured a law degree would allow me to save money by writing my own pre-nuptial agreement. Then I realized if I got a good MBA, then I could marry some rich broad with more money than me and I wouldn't need to have a pre-nuptial agreement, so getting a law degree would be silly. And that is why you must let me into the Harvard Business School.

Todd Allen

Donald Trump Will Steal Our Women

Beware, men of Chicago, a threatening situation lurks in our near future. A dastardly plan is in the offing that may be far beyond our capacity to deal with. It seems that the Chicago Sun-Times is selling their building. It will be torn down and a new building shall be erected in its place. As the Sun-Times building is hideously ugly, it might have the surface appearance of being a win-win situation. Instead, it may mess up our fun.

The new building, perhaps destined to be the tallest building in the world, is tentatively slated to be called "Trump Tower Chicago." That's right, Donald Trump is coming to town, and he's going to steal our women.

We shouldn't necessarily blame The Donald for what is sure to happen. It's not his fault he's going to steal our women. Well, not entirely. Still, this is going to be a problem. There's finite number of attractive women in Chicago. There are also a finite number of attractive women in New York City, where The Donald spends much of his time, but let's be honest here, the finite number in NYC threatens to become the infinity symbol when compared to Chicago. We're short on modeling agencies in this town. While The Donald has made his fair share of friends in NYC's pool of beauty, it's a big enough pool for people to share. We may not be so fortunate.

Oh, the rumors have started. You remember the Lincoln Park Trixie Society? (http://www.lptrixie.com) Chicago's society of social-climbing, marriage-hungry, young ladies? Word on the street is, the Trixies have already begun staking out Wabash Street, near the current site of the Sun-Times, hoping to catch The Donald unawares on his way to or from a business meeting. It will only get worse when construction begins. The Trixies are early adapters. The worst will come when The Donald makes good on his threat of making Chicago his second home.

Perhaps we shouldn't be too hard on The Donald. After all, he's a merely a stalking target for the Trixies. Just another piece of meat with a bank account. Still, the reality of the situation is grim for us normal Joe's. It cannot denied, not even by Monica Lewinsky, that fame, wealth and power can make a man attractive. The Donald has been able to stand out in these areas in a city that boasts much more of each than Chicago has hosted, well, at least since Michael Jordan started spending more time in Washington, D.C. and fell out of quite so public a view. It wouldn't be so bad if The Donald was a bad interview and lacking witty repartee, but such is not our luck. The Donald has his charm, and without half trying shall become the center of attention, as we native males capture a larger and larger share of attention from Wisconsin tourists, instead of local, thinner, female establishment. Oh, the shame of it all.

What's a single man to do in the face of the unintentional war about to break out? Upgrade his wardrobe? Yeah, you're going to have a better suit than Donald Trump, right. Hit the gym more? It's not going to make you more famous. Learn to fake a French accent? Actually, that could work if you don't break character.

No, men of Chicago, we have but one real hope. We must convince The Donald to bring women with him from New York. Much like the laws of wildlife conservation, we must enact legislation that for every woman he removes from our sphere of influence, he must replace her with another from the Big Apple.

Write your city alderman, today. It's our only hope.

Todd Allen

The Apartment Credit Check of Doom

I decided my landlord was raising the rent more than my place was worth. Come to find out they'd been hiking my rent much more than other, nicer buildings. It seems with Chicago's recent rise in unemployment, some of the nicer buildings aren't raising their rent as much, anymore. One of the buildings I looked at is considered by some to be Chicago's premiere address for a non-condo. I remembered a consultant I used to work with 4 years ago had lived there. Specifically, I remember him complaining about how much his rent was and thinking that the price was outlandishly expensive. Obviously, the price came down a little.

When I walked up to the building, it was mid-afternoon on a Sunday, and there was a stream of people with luggage getting into cabs. By the look of them, consultants heading towards the airport. Not a great surprise, as this building has a reputation for consultants living there. I took a look around and decided the apartment they showed me was a little smaller than what I wanted, but it was surprisingly cheap rent for the quality of the building, so I decided I'd take an application in case nothing better turned up. I can't believe I kept my eyes in their sockets when I looked at the application.

You may recall I'd made a comment about consultants living in the building. Well, the consulting industry in Chicago had a rough year. A lot of people got laid off. A lot of firms went out of business, not just small ones, either. A big firms like March First bit the dust, too. I don't know if that's what happened to this building. All I know is they had a separate attachment on "Leasing Qualifications and Requirements" that suggests to my untrained eye that this building got burned badly by several someones.

The qualifications were really all about credit and employment. The first thing that really made me raise an eyebrow was the clause that rent couldn't exceed 30% of your gross monthly income. That may be old hat to New Yorkers, but let me tell you, that just doesn't happen in Chicago. Even my realtor had never heard of a clause like that in Chicago before.

But wait, it gets better. How to verify income? Well, there's always a note from your employer. Or you can use your prior year's tax return. But wait, there's a clause on that. This building, should you opt for the tax return, wants you to get a note from your accountant, on your accountant's letterhead, with your account's CPA State ID #, saying that it really is your tax return.

I guess if you did your own taxes, you wouldn't be able to rent at this building?

Kinda makes you wonder if they had a problem with bogus tax returns accompanying lease applications, doesn't it?

But wait, we're not done with personal credit yet.

Should you have a Trust Fund, alimony, or the like, you need a verification of income for it. OK, I've met a few Trust Fund Babies that might lie about their Trust Fund, but, really, if I was the landlord of a Trust Fund Baby, I'd be more worried about what percentage of income was spent on party supplies.

Nobody with judgments, liens or bankruptcies in the last three years is welcome.

Finally, they want to verify you have an "80%" favorable credit rating fro one of the credit bureaus. Where did that come from? That's the first time I've seen a published minimum credit rating on a lease before, and my realtor almost fell over when she saw that, so it must've been pretty unusual and somewhat high.

So I really had to ask myself what kind of posers had lost their apartments when the rent came due? Obviously, a set of stringent requirements like that didn't material out of thin air.

And it gets better.

Yes, boys and girls, there are qualifications for corporate apartments, too. To look at the requirements, I'd guess they got burned even worse by a corporation or two, than by individual renters.

For a corporation to rent an apartment, they want a credit report from Dunn and Bradstreet, which I suppose is a normal thing to want.

Then they want three current trade references. Further, they want name, address and phone number for those trade references. I can't figure out if this is to see if the corporation ever pays its bills or to see if the corporation actually has any clients. I can think of a few high-profile start-ups that went out of business without having three clients.

Then they want an "Officer of the Company" to sign the lease and send a letter (on letterhead, naturally) stating who's supposed to be living in the apartment and who's supposed to be getting the invoices. Gee, you think maybe they had a couple squabbles about who was supposed to be paying the rent?

E-Mail From Nigeria

I'm not saying all this paperwork smacks of paranoia. Just that where there's smoke, there's usually fire. Kinda makes a fellow wonder what kind of people were showboating around the fancy housing to cause all that red tape to pop up?

Todd Allen

Layoffs Hit Another Service Sector: Crystal Consulting

(Chicago, IL) As the economy continues to retract, layoffs in the service sector have become regular occurrences. With staff cuts at traditional consulting firms like Anderson and the downfall of newcomers like MarchFirst, industry analysts have predicted job-cuts for similar companies, but a fresh round of cuts has caught forecasters by surprise.

"I think everyone in the business saw it coming," said Gastina Holohek, a Crystal consultant, formerly with Madame Zelda's Crystal Consulting and Tarot Analysis.

Nationwide, it is estimated some 1500 Crystal consultants have been laid off in the past two weeks.

"When revenues decline, consultants are among the first cuts to be made," explained Marsha Applebaum, a senior analyst with investment firm Goldsmith Sax. "Crystal consulting, while not always publicly associated with firms like McKinsey & Company, is still a method of strategic consulting, which is one of the first services to be cut during a recession."

While Crystal consulting is suffering losses, allied sectors are experiencing some short terms gains.

"While we're no longer retaining a Crystal consultant," stated Alexi Smith, president of Evanston, IL – based Squid Online Brokers, "we have established a working relationship with an astrologer. We find it very important to have strategic advice, and astrology is much less expensive."

E-Mail From Nigeria

Smith is not alone in seeking cheaper strategic advice. Much as larger corporations may drop a Big 5 consulting firm for the lower billing rates of an independent agency, many firms are looking into other sources of strategy with less inherent overhead.

Crystal consulting is a much more expensive business than are related industries, such as Numerology, Astrology, and Tarot consulting. The added expense comes from the cost of the crystals used in the business, which, according to industry sources, can be excessive. Numerology and Astrology consulting, while less expensive, still charge more than the Tarot industry, owing to the intense mathematical training undergone by their consultants.

Analysts predict the increase of business for Crystal consulting's related industries will be short lived in the case of Numerology and Astrology, but that the trickle down effect of cost cutting by clients should make up for natural attrition for the Tarot industry.

While the Crystal consultants retrain to handle a deck of cards, instead of crystals, dissension has started to rear its ugly head in the prediction-based strategy area. The Tea Leaves Readers Union has accused its competitors of posting false statements about the value of their services to Internet message boards targeting the business community.

"I think the petty jealousy caused by our more economical service is a disgrace to our market," Union Spokesman Domingo Saprona said in a prepared statement. "The leaves tell us who did it, so there can be no doubt, but this bitterness is bad for business."

Industry workers insist that their market will rise again and that analysts neither understand the nature of their nature of their work, nor are the qualified to predict the prediction business.

Todd Allen

Avoiding The Ex-Boss, An Exercise In Espionage

Ever have an old acquaintance that you just really didn't want to talk to? Somebody obtuse enough that it's just an altogether better thing to avoid all contact, than to get dragged down into the morass of their psyche?

I had something happen to me, a couple months back, and all those Mission: Impossible re-runs I've watched sure came in handy.

I was sitting in a trade association meeting when a former editor walked in. The people at the meeting shifted a little bit. I wasn't the only one who didn't want to talk to him. This former editor, we'll call him 'Irving," walked into the meeting a few minutes after it started, which for him is actually quite early. He has a reputation for being at least half an hour late and always makes a big show about arriving.

I'd been avoiding Irving for quite some time. I'd switched publications away from him, some six months prior, due to general distaste for his increasingly negative editorializing and concerns that he was going to turn into a lawsuit magnet. Indeed, this turned out to be a valid concern, as I've seen one Word file named "Complaint For Injunctive and Other Relief" which was labeled as though it had been filed in Circuit Court and with phrases like "defamation, per se" and "false light" being the counts defined by the document. He'd also had a couple temper tantrums about my departure in his publication after I'd left, and his reputation had gotten to the point that my former association with him was causing problems with clients. Given his propensity to get overly emotional, scream at people when upset, and then write about it for weeks on end in his publication, it just made more sense to stay out of sight and out of mind, than to confront him and give him more material to write about.

Normally, avoiding him wasn't a problem, as Irving has very poor eyesight. How poor? Well, he tends to examine nametags with a magnifying glass, although there's some conjecture that he spends more time examining women's nametags, given where women wear their nametags...

Suffice to say, he's been at several events, asking where I've disappeared to, and all the time, I've been 10 feet away. Considering the absurdity of the situation, it's like having the National Enquirer hire an irritable Jerry Lewis to follow me around. The problems I share with George Clooney, really...

Unfortunately, this was a small room, and I didn't have much space to maneuver. As the meeting went on, Irving decided to yell out the name of someone in attendance whose company had gone out of business 6 days prior, and made a snide remark about it for the whole room to hear. Seeing Irving was in the mood to cause a scene, not that it was unusual, deepened my sinking feeling.

Soon, Irving got up and started going around the room, seeing who was there and demanding they give him business cards.

One person, fearing a confrontation, covered up his nametag. This guy's boss removed some advertising from Irving's publication and Irving had been in a virtual vendetta ever since, writing nasty things about the boss in his publication and causing public scenes at similar events. The poor guy was afraid what would happen if Irving saw what company he was with.

Not really feeling like being made part of a spectacle and not having any place to disappear to, I only had one option open to me: disguise.

My hair was a bit longer than the last time Irving had spoke to me, and I figured it was time to take advantage of that. I took off my glasses, brushed my bangs down and pushed the hair brushed behind my ears to in front of my ears, basically going for something closer to the hippie look.

Irving sauntered over to me and asked who I was.

"Nobody important," I said quietly, looking down.

"Can you tell me what company you're with," Irving asked, surprisingly politely.

"Oh, I'm not really here."

After that, Irving announced to the room, during speaker Q&A, mind you, that there were people there who don't want anyone to know what companies they were with. Not that Irving could tell the difference between not wanting people to know and people just not telling him.

Irving went on, collecting cards, oblivious to who he'd been talking to. At this point, the fellow who was covering up his nametag was endangering his life, suppressing both breathing and laughter after witnessing my ruse, half in disbelief that I pulled it off.

I talked to some people I needed to talk to, and walked between rooms, making sure my disguise was intact, since I wasn't sure where Irving had wandered off to. Sure enough, it's well that I did, for at that moment (as two people later informed me), Irving was inquiring as to who I was, and, unfortunately, some weasel had told him. I saw him start to come out of the room and kept walking straight ahead down the hall.

"Who are you, mystery man," Irving called after me.

"No one important," I said and started walking a little faster. I'd avoided having him go off on me for damn near 6 months, and I wasn't looking to end the streak.

"Are you Todd Allen," he yelled.

"Nope," I said and spotted an elevator.

As I jumped into the elevator, I could hear Irving and his cane, shuffling down the hall as quickly as he could, trying to catch and confront me.

The elevator was full, with roughly five women in their 30s, presumably finishing up an evening MBA class, since this happened in a college building. They looked a little disturbed by all the commotion, and they were holding the door open.

"It's a former employer," I attempted to explain. "He's still bitter."

The door still wasn't closer and Irving's cane was making a lot of noise.

"Is that Todd Allen?" He yelled in the hallway.

"OK, this door needs to close now," I said, as the women in the elevator got even more nervous.

Finally, the door started closing, and the noise of the cane was almost on top of the elevator. The door had been open long enough the buzzer started to sound. I personally helped the extremely slow door close, as the sound of the cane stopped in front of the door, which I can only assume shut in Irving's face.

"You weren't kidding," one of the women said, in reference to my comment about bitterness, and thus I made my escape.

Oh yes, Irving's been whining about the event in his publication for a couple months now, but at least I didn't have to listen to him complain, and, as of this writing, I still don't think he knows what really happened.

E-Mail From Nigeria

Terror Grips McCormick As Local Publisher Tries To Drive

(Chicago, IL) In places like Beirut, a jeep speeding towards a building can cause great fear. On September 18, at the ITECH trade show at McCormick Place in Chicago, it wasn't a speeding jeep, it was a speeding golf cart.

Somehow, Irving, owner of a local gossip publication and noted loudmouth, was able to commandeer a vehicle resembling a golf cart, to traverse, indeed, zip through, the aisles of the ITECH trade show as he demanded to know who people were and that they give him their business cards. Irving's poor eyesight is a running joke in certain parts of Chicago's technology community, as are his much self-hyped medical treatments for his eyes.

In addition to not really being able to see very well, Irving is also well known for not driving, having regularly coerced people into driving him to events, occasionally, the event sponsors, themselves.

So you might be wondering if it's a good idea to give a man, with vision problems and little-to-no experience driving, a golf cart and turn him loose in a crowded room. And you would be correct to be concerned.

Instead of a speeding jeep heading towards a building, there was a speeding golf cart heading towards a booth. It seems Irving physically ran into the Illinois Department of Commerce and Community Affairs (DCCA) booth.

Witnesses say that Irving had finished yelling at a speaker and was attempting to do what sounds like a three-point turn with his cart. While backing up, Irving, who apparently did not look behind himself first, (the cart did not have a rearview mirror) collided with a portion of the DCCA booth containing a television display. The cart struck the booth below the speakers and failed to cause any serious damage. Fortunately, no one was injured during the collision.

DCCA staff members were somewhat unnerved by the experience. This is somewhat understandable, as Irving is a frequent critic of their department. While government buildings downtown are flanked by concrete barriers to prevent terrorists from driving cars into them, the DCCA staff was forced to improvise, placing large potted plants on either side of the display, where it might be more vulnerable to ramming. They also turned up the volume on the television, in hopes that future drivers might hear the television, even if they couldn't see it. A staff member commented that while a wire from the ceiling stabilized the display, they hadn't built the booth to survive a collision by a 300-pound man in a tricked-out golf cart. Still, they bravely carried on activities at the booth, in the wake of the incident.

Indignant Online hopes, in the future, McCormick officials will not give high-speed vehicles to people to whom the question "how close is he to legally blind" is a legitimate question, or at least provide such individuals with a trained driver.

E-Mail From Nigeria

Enron: The Circle-Jerk Of Backstabbing

The really odd thing about the whole Enron collapse is how where one hand would normally be washing the other, that one hand is instead busy stabbing the other in the back.

Consider the politicians. It's well documented how millions of dollars went to campaign contributions to various political parties and candidates, with not an insignificant sum going to current President George W. Bush. Let's not be naïve about the nature of campaign contributions. I live in Chicago, and it's pretty obvious who's been donating what around here, if you know what I mean, especially if there are Real Estate developers involved. There's one particular alderman that could probably fiscally benefit by just being open about it and placing his influence on eBay. Make sure he's getting a fair market value and all. Enron paid their money, and it sounds like they got in on some meetings. Likely, they got a little say in the development of some energy policies, although the powers that be deny.

What nobody denies, is that when the chips were down, Enron attempted to make some phone calls and call in some favors for all those donations. Their political buddies left them out to dry.

While it's always refreshing to see politicians develop ethics somewhere along the line, it doesn't change the fact that they left their donating friends for dead. Such is never the intention of people donating in the 7-figure area. Politicians that don't know the score when they accept that kind of money? That would be a figment of someone's imagination. Whoops, the hand the usually washes had a knife. How unusual. Plenty of grist for the proponents of campaign reform that the politicians don't want anyway.

Consider the Enron employees. Granted, they got screwed unbelievably hard on the stocks, among other things. Still, I can't walk the 10 feet outside my building to buy the morning paper without tripping over some Enron employee (or is that ex-employee) trying to blow the whistle after the fact. Now I'm sure there were a couple of people legitimately concerned about what was going on, but this is getting ridiculous. Look, Chicken Little, the sky has already fallen, so are you just covering your ass or trying to twist the knife in your boss, a little more? Fortunately, there are some people richly deserving of knife twisting on the receiving end, but you can't tell me this was a company composed entirely of angels. Nope, the breach of trust flows both ways.

Consider Star Wars. Yes, it appears the higher-ups at Enron sought to use the Force, even if it ended up more Farce than Force. Enron was concealing their debt with a company called "Joint Energy Development Investments" or JEDI, if you prefer. They had another company called Chewco, which is a little too close to Chewbacca for the liking of many Star Wars fans. It's bad enough you have to manipulate the status of your debt, but maligning the memories of films that a goodly number of people live by? That's another stab in the back. Why couldn't they have named it Jar-Jar? A bad joke of a character for a bad joke of a company makes more sense to me. In a related note, no Jurassic Park fans seem to be upset that Enron has been linked to another company called Raptor. I wonder what the NBA thinks about that?

Finally, we have good old Arthur Andersen Consulting, the bean counters that signed off on all the questionable financial statements. And judging by the number of federal investigations, it looks like there may be some criminal wrong-doings with that accounting, and maybe

E-Mail From Nigeria

some of the consultants will be sharing jail sell with Enron management. Suits me, since my experience with Andersen consultants has been that they're as arrogant as they are inexperienced, but I guess they must have some employees hidden somewhere that have been out of a school for more than a year and a half, and actually completed a project before, right? Maybe I just haven't met them.

No, for all the backstabbing Andersen's accounting did to the employees and investors, Andersen may have had the most loyalty to their real client, the Enron executives who signed their checks. Even after the scandal broke, Andersen kept on shredding those accounting documents. Destroy any evidence you can, now that could be construed as a true act of loyalty.

For all the circular treachery swimming around in this scandal, isn't it ironic that it's the outside consultant that acts with the most loyalty? And isn't it nice to know you can count on a Big 5 consulting firm to demonstrate loyalty, especially when they're doing it for all the wrong reasons?

Good luck in prison, kids.

Todd Allen

Aerobics For A 5-Year-old? Marketing to Crazed, Over-Weight Suburbanites

Ever see those annoying "Power Pumper 2000" ads on television? You know, the Big Wheel-looking kiddie tricycle substitute, with the over-enthusiastic mommies fawning over its effectiveness for burning calories?

And you might ask yourself whether this product was created to be enjoyed by children, or to play on the neuroses of those children's parents? Well, in fairness, the inventor might not have had the exact same marketing campaign in mind. Maybe the product is a joy for the kids to ride. I have no opinion on the product itself, just the implications of how they're selling it.

The thing that really gave me pause was when a borderline-white-trash mommy was talking about her offspring getting exercise and burning calories. When have you actually heard a parent concerned about how many calories their child was burning?

I thought, perhaps, I might be reading a little too much into the ads, so I went to their website at www.powerpumper.com. And lo, my suspicions were confirmed.

And I quote:

"It's been called a cross between a Big Wheel™ and Health Rider™."

E-Mail From Nigeria

Excuse me, but since it also says it's for the 5 – 11 year-old set, why are they describing it in terms of an adult fitness device often marketed as a weight loss device? Has little Johnny been eating too many biscuits?

But it gets more absurd:

"Its innovative, award-winning design promotes both lower and upper body exercise for a well-rounded workout even while your child is 'playing.'"

And am I to understand that children playing is not good enough? That a structured workout is necessary? That's a little on the obsessive-compulsive side, isn't it? Is baseball/softball an unworthy childhood past-time? Let's read on:

"Give your kids enjoyment and aerobics. Give yourself peace of mind."

Yes, obviously aerobics is peace of mind. If that's the case, why don't you have the kids join you with your Richard Simmons and Jane Fonda work-out tapes?

Do you get the feeling that the marketing geniuses behind this device are hoping that out of shape, flabby parents project their perceived inadequacies onto their children? I know, let's look at the testimonials page:

"I like the idea that he is burning calories rather than sitting in front of a game all day."

That quote being from the "Parents" section of ye olde testimonial page. Excuse me while I go vomit. Burning calories has now become the definition of childhood activity? Does anybody think like that?

I've got news for you, if the kid is overweight, yeah, the kid probably should be having a more active lifestyle, but the kid is probably eating too much, too. God forbid the baby boomers take a little responsibility for parenting.

No, instead we have a wonderful product that allows parents who have used and abused their bodies to take comfort in knowing that instead of experiencing the youthful joys of childhood play, their children are being tricked into exercising.

Now, if I just had a way to sell psychological counseling to the parents who are buying into this marketing approach, I could make some money, too.

P.T. Barnum would love those ads.

Oh yeah, let us not forget that at the bottom of their web page, Power Pumper (or should we say the Columbia-Inland corporation) has two products listed as "coming soon."

First, we have the Power Pumper, Jr., for ages 2-6, because every toddler wants an aerobic workout.

Then we have "Power Pumper – Adult." I guess it makes since they might want to have a product that the demographic they're marketing towards could use themselves, instead of exercising vicariously through their offspring.

I wonder what Freud would say about that group dynamic?

E-Mail From Nigeria

Secret Internet Crushes: Romance Or Trouble Coming Looking For You?

"Guess what... you've got a secret admirer!" Or so reads the e-mail CrushLink.com sends out.

"ATTENTION: This is not a gimmick. Someone (probably someone near you right now) has expressed a romantic interest in you. Don't hesitate. Find out who it is, and see if you're a match! It could change your life!"

Or so the e-mail continues to say.

CrushLink is a website that ostensibly allows you to give that special someone a hint that you like them. The way it works, is you register with the site, giving your name, e-mail address and date of birth. Then you type in the name and e-mail address of someone you have a crush on and hope they figure out you're the one with the crush on them and that they can also figure out which e-mail address you're using at the time.

Now if you're on the receiving end of one of these crushes, you get an e-mail as described above, with a membership code supposedly relating to your secret admirer. Once you register, you get a hint as to who your admirer might be. The hint could be an age range, the number of letters in the first or last name, and so on.

If you need more hints, you can either sign up for offers through the site or type in more names of people you have a crush on (the premise is theoretically for mutual crushes to meet). Of course, typing in random names increases the circles and away she goes.

Todd Allen

This is not entirely a good thing. Awhile back I got a secret crush in the e-mail. I went to the site and through various means prescribed by the site, obtained enough hints about the person who had a crush on me that I was able to narrow down the field.

I was given information like number of letters in the first name, number of letters in the last name, and the number of times certain letters occurred in the name. Enough information that I only knew three people that fit the criteria. One of them would have been a pleasant surprise, as I'd been blatantly flirting with her in the near past and I'd thought it hadn't worked out. Another of them would have been an uncomfortable situation. The third possibility was just a bad thing, should it have turned out to be true. Then again, it could have been a fourth young lady whose name just didn't register on my radar. Or, perhaps one of my friends was screwing with me.

It wasn't the first one. I called her described the hints I was given that matched her (as to not sound like a total loon), and she denied it. I also typed her e-mail in, to make sure she hadn't just gotten uncharacteristically shy, but it bounced back. The reason I talked to her first, is that anytime you make a guess, that person gets an e-mail. If the other person guesses your name, you both get an e-mail suggesting you get together.

That left me with a problem. If one of my other two candidates was interested in me, I really didn't want to have a third party, or a third party web site for that matter, shoehorn us into a get-together. Whichever of those parties it was, if I typed the wrong name, I could end up with someone I wasn't interested in thinking I was.

For that matter, if I was considering typing a name in, just because I was afraid someone undesirable had a crush, how am I to know that I didn't get my original e-mail because some lady thought "oh god, I hope Todd Allen doesn't have a crush on me," and typed my name in?

E-Mail From Nigeria

No, I think that secret online crushes are definitely more likely to get me in trouble than they are to hook me up. Although I'd like to think somewhere out in e-space, there's a pleasant young lady whose name I just couldn't recall, wondering why I never returned her crush... even if my brain tells me differently.

Todd Allen

If The Political Parties Hate Each Other So Much, Give Congress an Open-Mike Night

Ever watch C-SPAN on Sunday evenings? They show re-runs of "Question Time" for the House of Commons from British Parliament. It's a wacky format. The Prime Minister sits on one side of the room, with his party. The other party sits across the room from them and they spend most of the session just ripping on each other, under the pretense of asking the Prime Minister policy questions. It's great. One opposition party speaker asked the Prime Minister, straight out of the blue, if he could explain why worker productivity had gone down during his administration. Another speaker read the Prime Minister some contradictory letters from the P.M. about a health care initiative and asked if said P.M.'s promises were nothing more than rubbish. After the questions, the Prime Minister was allowed to answer, but it was really more a matter of making fun of those asking questions than really answering anything.

Essentially, it seems to be a game of verbal one-upsmanship combined with a slightly more issue-oriented version of street dissing (disrespecting). The object of the game seems to be to crack the wittiest accusation your opponent can't talk his way out of, and leave him looking like a laughing-stock dolt. It's pretty vicious.

As we witness the two parties, here in the U.S., sniping at each other in the name of a bi-partisanship movement, it's apparent both sides clearly despise each other too much to actually want a real debate (thank you, Newt Gingrich, for your lasting legacy), I'm thinking Congress ought to adapt this British practice, only instead of limiting the questioning to just the president, I think any member of Congress should be able to ask embarrassing questions to any other member, plus the president and vice-president. (Hey, you know this was the format Dan Quayle was born to be humiliated in.) Every couple of weeks, all the pissed off members of Congress could get in a (large) room and in an organized fashion, insult each other on policy issues to their hearts content. Get their aggressions out.

For instance, instead of saying, as the layman would address someone who'd annoyed him, "Yo mama's so ugly, she's got to pull the sheet over her head so sleep can sneak up on her," we could have someone asking Jesse Helms an ever so gentle question about the relationship between his voting record and campaign contributions from tobacco firms, or someone asking Joseph Lieberman about his sudden love-affair with Hollywood movie executives every since he started hanging out with Gore. The questions in the "Question Time" format always boil down to the same implications of a "yo mama" joke, that the target is a dim-wit of questionable character, and being that it's a group of politicians, the implications are likely true. You also get to see if any of the politicians are capable of thinking quickly enough to offer a snappy comeback. Wouldn't you like to have seen if Strom Thurmond still had his wits about him as he neared his 100th birthday?

In the case of Britain's Tony Blair, his comebacks tend to revolve around throwing statistics back at his accusers, and frankly the idea of Congressmen having to actually familiarize themselves with the facts of actual policy issues would be enough a reason to institute such an event. I know we've all had our doubts if our representation actually knew what time it was, and this would be a highly entertaining venue for discovery.

If we really wanted to do this right, we'd arrange for some commercial sponsors (proceeds to go to reducing the debt or getting a political science professor to explain to Tipper Gore that censorship is more of a fascist trait than a democratic/liberal trait) and get one conservative and one liberal comedian to act as moderator/hosts. Or just see what Jesse Ventura's doing that evening, since he'd probably get a kick out of laying into the entire political establishment, all at once.

Really, it's the same principle as Roman Gladiator games. Unleash all the hostilities with one event, and if somebody gets hurt, well, it's only a politician and they probably had it coming. In the meantime everyone else gets a show.

E-Mail From Nigeria

Women And Drinking

Todd Allen

E-Mail From Nigeria

Lingerie Shopping

"I promised this girl I'd buy her some lingerie," said the voice on the phone. "Would you come to Victoria's Secret with me while I pick something out?"

The voice on the other end of the phone was my buddy, Cussy. I found it quite comical that a man who enjoyed the company of women as much as Cussy would be nervous shopping for lingerie. I mean, really, what's so scary about women's underwear? (Well, actually, I suppose Rosanne Barr's underwear would probably scare me, but other than that...) I decided this was too good an opportunity to pass up. And besides, Cussy was admitting my superior knowledge of naughty nighties.

Cussy was so nervous about his shopping, he was actually having trouble deciding which Victoria's Secret he wanted to shop at, the one in Water Tower, or the stand-alone store across the street. I suggested a more upscale venue, but the nervous boy decided it would be more money than he wanted to spend. In the end, he decided the Water Tower store would be best, after all, it was a mall of sorts, and therefore, apparently, less of a stigma.

As we walked over, it came out that there were two different women Cussy was buying the lingerie for. He hadn't yet made up his mind which one of them would receive the gift, although he'd only promised it to one. Still, he thought they probably both wore the same size, and being a fiscal conservative, he figured his investment could produce a dividend with either prospective paramour. It seems my enterprising friend had many things on his mind, and I was sure I was going to enjoy what would happen next.

We stood outside Victoria's Secret and Cussy stared inside, with some trepidation. I glanced at him, snickered, boldly walked in and gestured for him to follow. Seeing two men walk in, which I'm sure generally means assistance is needed, a lovely young clerk appeared, almost out of thin air.

"Can I help you?" she asked me in a voice far too innocent for someone that sells provocative undergarments.

"No," I replied. "But he needs lots of help."

I turned and pointed to Cussy. I assure you, Indians can blush. And he was glowing like a Rudolph the Red-Nosed Reindeer.

The clerk, obviously accustomed to jittery men venturing in, asked Cussy a few questions about what he wished to purchase. Unfortunately, he had no idea what he wanted to purchase. He gestured to me, so I told the clerk he was probably wanting a teddy or a nightie for his little friend. Cussy nodded his head in agreement. I found it quite disturbing that after all his bravado, he seemed not to be too familiar with what the ladies were wearing. Either he must take off his glasses too soon, or he fancies himself a racecar driver.

The clerk showed him a teddy and asked him if that was what he sought. He turned to me and asked my opinion.

"That's sheer," I said, holding my hand underneath it to demonstrate the effect. "If she put it on, you'd see right through it, and you'd lose all control. You don't want that."

The clerk was barely able to suppress a giggle, but persevered on, showing Cussy four or five other offerings, before she posed a question to him.

"Do you know what size she wears," the clerk quite innocently inquired.

E-Mail From Nigeria

"Yes," I said with an edge in my voice, a wide grin enveloping my face. "That's a very good question."

Cussy seemed on the verge of breaking a sweat. He glanced at me, finally realizing that bringing a noted smart ass like myself along might not have been the brightest idea he ever had. He glanced back at the clerk, who wasn't sure why he was tensing up so suddenly.

"Um," Cussy began, trying to regain his composure. "She's about your size. Maybe a little smaller."

"Well," began the clerk, addressing Cussy as though she was explaining something to a small child. "I wear a size 6. Do you know what her actual size is?"

"Um," Cussy had officially broken a sweat. He glanced at me, noted the evil grin on my face grown so large, it threatened to block out the sun, and then glanced back at the clerk. "Um, um... 'B'?"

Now it was the clerk's turn to look disturbed. The only thing I could do to keep from laughing at him, which wouldn't have been fair to the poor clerk, was to turn away. The clerk politely excused herself. We did not encounter her again.

"What did I say?" was his exasperated plea.

"She asked you for a dress size," I said. "10 is a dress size. You said 'B.' 'B' is the cup part of a bra size. For instance, 40D is a bra size. She doesn't think you know the difference between a dress and a bra. Oh, yeah, you weren't staring at her breasts when you said she was the same size as your little friend, were you?"

Cussy, realizing what he'd just done, let off a blue streak as I proceeded to laugh.

Realizing that we probably weren't going to be getting any more assistance from the store staff, I pointed out a couple of fairly conservative nighties that might be appropriate to give someone he hadn't known very long, as not to offend them, when they were already exhibiting questionable judgment by associating with him, and he didn't want to push his luck. After deliberating over how little he wanted to spend, Cussy picked one, a different clerk rang him up, and we departed.

Once we were out of the store, his composure returned.

"I don't know what I was thinking," he growled at me. "That's the last time I ever ask you to help me buy something for a woman."

Then again, he later had me help him pick out flowers, but that's another story.

And for the record, to the best of my recollection, the nightie Cussy bought found never made it to either of the women he had in mind while we were shopping. Fortunately, it still fit contestant #3.

E-Mail From Nigeria

Losing A Girl To Your Clone

Looking for a change of pace, a buddy and myself ventured into the drinking establishments of Lincoln Park, a particularly yuppified neighborhood of Chicago famed for its particularly mercenary young female denizens, affectionately known as the "trixies." (See http://www.lptrixie.com for the trixies in all their glory.) We didn't merely find a change of pace; we found that reality is stranger than fiction as our evening veered into what easily could have been an episode of Seinfeld.

The evening had started innocently enough, but shortly after entering our second stop of the evening, chaos struck. It began innocently enough. A little blonde trixie tried to bum a smoke off us. Strange thing was, she wouldn't go away when we identified ourselves as non-smokers. Now normally, neither of us are the type to summarily dismiss an interested young lovely, but this trixie was so dizzy as to have trouble standing, couldn't make conversation about anything besides the cancer sticks she was lacking and wasn't even coherent on the subject of tobacco (attempted topics included smoking as a social addiction and why she couldn't just stop cold turkey). In short, her vacuous chatter about her attempts to contract cancer was disturbing our ability to enjoy our beer, a cardinal sin for a young lovely on a Friday night. After a few minutes, I was finally able to get rid of her, after telling her about my grandfather losing 3/4 of a lung to smoking.

We breathed a sigh of relief, went back to our beers and noticed the trixie return with a freshly purchased pack of smokes a few minutes later, prompting my buddy to remark on the vapidness of trying to bum smokes off a couple obvious non-smokers when she could just buy the silly things, herself. This was when she came back and tried to talk to us again. No, that's not entirely true. She came back and tried to talk to my buddy, who promptly rebuffed her and her constant chattering about smoking.

"That was strange," he said to me.

"Dude," I replied. "She was talking to you, not me. I think she wants you."

We looked up and, son of a gun, she hadn't gone back to the group of people she'd entered with. Instead, she was hovering a couple tables away, staring at my sidekick.

"I think you're right," my startled friend stammered.

"I take it I'm getting another beer and staying here awhile," I inquired.

My buddy added that I should also be getting him a drink, and to try and figure out if the young lady was with someone, as we'd both thought we'd seen her hanging on someone earlier. After a few minutes, she returned to her entourage and draped herself over a boy. Eventually, the boy turned around to where we could get a good look at him. The results were disturbing, to say the least.

You may recall, in the Superman comic books, there was an attempt to clone Superman, which yielded Bizarro, Superman's imperfect duplicate? Well, the trixie appeared to be attached to my buddy's imperfect clone. The trixie's boy had the same build of my friend, the same complexion, the same height, similar glasses, the same color of hair with a similar, yet sloppy, cut and ditto for the similar, but unkempt, goatee. The trixie's boy also appeared to be 10 years my buddy's junior. In short, the trixie was slithering over a younger, dorkier version of my friend, who was starting to go into shock.

E-Mail From Nigeria

"That guy looks like me," he managed to get out.

"Yup," I agreed. "But he's young and sloppy. I think she wants to trade up for the mature model. That's why she's been circling you all night."

My buddy, clearly unnerved by the boyfriend's physical resemblance, mumbled something about not wanting to start trouble if the trixie was indeed there with someone. Knowing the materialistic nature of trixies, and that my buddy's law degree would likely be considered more desirable than his clone's apparent unfamiliarity with a beard-trimmer, I assured him, should he talk to the young lady, no one would get close enough to lay a hand on him. Besides, the clone had been ignoring said trixie the entire evening and she'd been the one coming around, looking to move up dating ladder.

Alas, as I said this, the trixie's group departed and, after briefly pausing to glance back at my buddy with what appeared to be a tinge of regret, she left with the clone.

Perhaps my friend should have said something to her a bit sooner, but I don't blame him for being shaken. It's not too often you run into someone who's your body double and it's unheard of to run into a body double and have their woman make a pass at you.

I ask you, what could be stranger than losing a girl to your imperfect, dorky clone?

Todd Allen

Call Her Within Five Business Days Or I Take Her Number Back

Ever have too many women banging down your door? Puzzled with what to do with all the phone numbers you're getting from single girls? One of my buddies was so over-extended, he's been loaning out phone numbers.

So my buddy is in a club in New York. One of his friends is visiting. The fellow visiting is engaged, and the rumor that someone is about to be married is making the rounds through the dance floor. Not that people enjoy being the last fling with someone preparing to take the death march down the aisle of matrimony, but a young lovely, under the unbelievably wrong impression that my buddy is the one that's getting married, asks him to dance.

"Are you the one who's engaged," she asked him as they slinked to the dance floor.

"No," he replied. "But I'd like to be."

The silly little thing bought his line (nobody said club girls weren't occasionally gullible). At the end of the evening, after a few more statements about lasting relationships that might be more fiction than fact, my buddy was presented with her home phone number, office phone number, mailing address, street address and probably a couple other ways to contact her, just so he'd have no excuse if he didn't.

E-Mail From Nigeria

Now while most guys would be happy at this concerted show of interest, my buddy's reaction was lukewarm. It seems his dance card for the following week was already filled up. Don't ask me why, but he just had too many women making demands on his time. Understanding that a phone number from a willing and attractive young lady really wasn't something to be squandered, he approached one of his comrades, who was going through, shall we say, a dry spell.

"I am loaning you this number," he said as he placed the card in his friend's hand. "You have five business days in which to use it. I am doing this, because I don't have time to see her this week and I remember what it's like to be hard up. If you have not used this card by next Monday, I am repossessing it."

"But Monday is a holiday" his friend stammered. "That's only four business days."

"You need an extension," my buddy sneered. "Fine. But you better call her by Tuesday or I'm taking her number back and calling her myself."

"So what are you going to say to her," a third member of the party asked. "Hi. You were hitting on my friend at the club last weekend and he didn't have time to call you this week, so he loaned me your number?"

The face of my buddy's friend turned a couple interesting colors, but he didn't answer.

Then, satisfied that he'd arranged for his latest admirer to be taken care of, at least until he could find time on his calendar to attend to her himself, my buddy got into a cab and went home.

We should all have such busy schedules.

Todd Allen

Another Tale Of Money-Hungry Lincoln Park Girls

I had a Trixie moment, this weekend. Those of you not living in Chicago, may not be familiar with the Trixies. Head over to http://lptrixie.com for a look at the Lincoln Park Trixie Society, a satirical tribute to the social climbing, marriage-minded, money-hungry young ladies that seem to flock to the upwardly-mobile neighborhood of Lincoln Park. Or to put in plain English, we're talking about gold-diggers, and I don't mean Dean Martin's old back-up singers. That site documents, and doesn't really exaggerate the phenomenon.

So I decide I haven't done a Lincoln Park pub crawl in a while and head over to a bar that's a few blocks off the trashy-trendy Lincoln Avenue strip. Lincoln Avenue has morphed into something I hardly recognize anymore. Let's just put it this way, I recently had it pointed out to me, the reason I was no longer enjoying one of my normal Lincoln Park pub crawl stops, was that the clientele had changed. I didn't believe her when she told me, but sure enough, next time I stopped at the place, pretty much everybody that wasn't in a group of three or more was gay. My friend told me this establishment had taken to having some sort of "show tune" event on Sundays to counter the other bars football programming. I'm guessing the patron shift was a result. It still was a mixed room, but it was all too clear where the singles scene in the room was heading. Let's just say I pounded my Guinness and left before somebody tried to buy me a drink.

Avoiding the Lincoln strip, I enter one of the last taverns in the area that hadn't gotten too trashy, and proceed to the back bar. The place is entirely too full, and has a gender ratio with entirely too many men. There weren't any stools, but I was able to belly up to the bar in an area that at least had a few women in it. As I sipped my Guinness, I noticed something odd: wristbands. Most of the people in the back room had wristbands on, like there was some sort of party going on, except nobody challenged me when I entered the back room, so either it wasn't a private function, or I was just too pretty to be turned away. I'm thinking it had more to do with my money being green.

While I was trying to figure out if I was crashing a party for a bunch of kids from DePaul University (The doorman had told me my driver's license was "a beauty," which is funny, since women keep freaking out that I'm not in my mid-30s and some doorman thinks I'm a minor with a good fake ID.) or if I've landed smack dap in the lap of a Trixie party, one of the young lovelies starts going from table to table with a camera, and it became very obvious she was only stopping at the table that had couples at them. Lessee, I'm in Lincoln Park, there's a group of, say 30 couples with wristbands in a bar, and some chick is taking pictures of all the couples. If this were an episode of "Lost in Space," the Robot would be waving its arms and saying "Warning, Trixie presence. Danger, Will Robinson."

As if on cue, a blonde comes up to camera girl and informs her that a boy she obviously is interested in, is thinking about leaving. He'll get another picture, but only if it's Bass. Otherwise, he was leaving. Something had to be done, immediately.

Just like a Trixie. Free drinks were leaving, and presumably he hadn't had enough to take Trixie #2 home with him. Tell you the truth, I think they were more concerned about not getting another pitcher out of the guy. I mean, only one girl could get her hooks in him, but everybody could drink his pitcher. You can't spit in Lincoln Park, without hitting one of these Trixies, which reminds me, next time I'm in Lincoln Park, I need to spit more often.

Still, we would be remiss, not to comment on the little Lincoln Park Meal-Ticket, whose beer (and probably salary, as well) Trixie #2 desired. If somebody orders a pitcher and you don't like the beer in it, order your own damn drink. Anybody with half a spine can do that. What kind of a jackass pouts and threatens to leave if everyone won't drink his brand? If the bar didn't stock Bass, I can understand wanting to leave. I've left bars before, when establishments have had an inadequate selection of beverages. No, he may have been wearing a target on his chest from the minute he walked in the room, but this guy was Trixie-bait at heart.

Such a predictable evening for the area.

And people wonder why I don't live in Lincoln Park...

E-Mail From Nigeria

My Tourist Buddy And His Failed Fling

So one of my old buddies pops into town for the weekend. Aggressive New Yorker that he is, he had to make a big deal out of being in town, throw a little money around, see the sites, terrorize the locals. You know, play at being a tourist.

The sort of thing did we do? Go into a fancy store like Hermes (VERY expensive French clothes), so he can get a bribe, I mean gift, for some business acquaintance that did him a favor. Why is that considering terrorizing? Well, while my buddy was dressed formally, I wore a loud Hawaiian shirt under my dark blazer, so that we might see the startled look on the clerk's face as I examined the ties a tad theatrically and my buddy referred to my expertise in matters of fashion etiquette and pondered what he should buy for a CFO, as if my opinion should be definitive. If you walk in dressed down and have some vague clue what you're looking at, people wonder exactly how rich you must be (and if you wear really ugly clothes, they'll think its designer fashions). It works every time, too, although I prefer a two-day beard and a bright orange, old school Tampa Bay Buccaneers sweatshirt to create optimal confusion for highbrow clerks.

And as things tend to happen when people suddenly appear in town, some things get all messed up.

For instance, my buddy's new shoes. Throwing around some money (after all, Chicago isn't as expensive as New York), my buddy went to an Italian designer shop, that shall remain nameless to wallow in their own embarrassment, and bought himself a pair of shoes. When we got back to my crash pad, for my buddy had commandeered my living room floor (he'd need to lose a little weight before he could commandeer the couch), he tried put on the new shoes, only to discover they'd put the wrong size shoes in the box. His vengeance for that would come the next day.

At the time I was busy trying to find something to put on the living room floor for him to sleep on. As I'd been abducted to terrorize boutique owners with him, I hadn't gotten a chance to acquire the air mattress he was to crash on, and it didn't look like we'd have time to grab it before his nightlife commitments were due. Or, as I said to my friend with the air mattress, "let me see if I get this straight: you're going to leave the air mattress with your doorman, and at 3am, after a full night of partying, I'm going to go up to your doorman and tell him you've left a mattress for me to pick up?" She said she hadn't thought of it that way, but it was the plan.

So things got a little more messed up, but that was a minor issue. My buddy had managed to get himself double-booked, without even being in the city for even 5 hours. He had to see a business associate to drop off a bribe, er, gift and he also had to see a young lady who had requested his presence. It was decided we should visit the business associate first, and then follow the young lady to the club where all the pretty people go. Thus, it was necessary for the young lady to meet us where I lived, so that we might coordinate schedules and not get lost.

I gave the young lady very precise directions on how to get to my address. She followed them, but couldn't find my building. She called my buddy's cell phone and said she could find the address, because "all the buildings down here are big." Now you're thinking this girl might not be very bright, just now noticing that there are a lot of tall buildings in downtown Chicago. You'd be right, but you'd be over-estimating the poor dear's intellectual capacity.

E-Mail From Nigeria

When we went downstairs, she was actually parked in front of my building. If she'd gone forward, maybe 15 feet, she'd have driven through the front door. At best, you could say she was unaware of her surroundings. At worst, she wasn't even intelligent enough to read the street address off a building. But wait, it gets better.

When we went downstairs, she was in her car, with the window rolled down, talking to a man. In the time it took us to catch the elevator, she had managed to have two men try to pick her up... and she did all this while sitting in her car. Not standing in front of the building, but while seated in her car. Further, she was convinced one of the men was actually a pimp who was trying to recruit her into his stable. First off, I find it highly unlikely a pimp would be recruiting hookers in front of my building. Second off, how in God's name does a woman manage to attract a pimp while sitting in her car, talking on a cell phone?

I fear my buddy's female acquaintance would lose a game of tic tac toe to a box of rocks, if you get my drift.

It was decided that the young lady would not accompany us to have a drink with my buddy's business acquaintance. Probably a good idea, because if she said even once sentence, or mentioned trying to find my apartment building, it would be pretty obvious there could be only one reason my buddy had her in tow.

As we drove to the first stop, I recounted to my buddy how his little blonde friend seemed very concerned I should be going to the pretty people's club... almost as if she'd wanted him to herself. I told him I thought it would be best if I removed myself from the situation and went to my normal watering hole. I figured he could call me and let me know if he was still crashing at my place or not. He said she'd asked similarly transparent questions to him, subtle and understated thing that she wasn't, and he thought it was probably a good idea for me to bail. We agreed he had until 2:30 am to contact me at my normal watering hole, otherwise I would assume him AWOL and he was on his own. Truthfully, I didn't expect to hear from him again until the next day.

So I went to my normal watering hole and dutifully BEHAVED for an extended period of time, while waiting to find out if I was still managing a flophouse for the evening. Behaving yourself on a Saturday night is easier said than done, I might add. Sure enough, around 2am, I received a call at the bar. The little soldier had struck out. How you strike out with someone that bubble-headed and intent on getting you alone is beyond me. He mumbled something about her deciding halfway through the evening that she actually liked him. As she seemed to put a gaping lack of forethought into her actions and had arbitrarily changed to the happy homemaker tract, I can understand why one might seek domestic bliss with someone a bit more... what is the term? Cognizant? Stable? Awake?

So, at 3 in the morning, I collected an air mattress from my friend's doorman. My buddy, being a very lazy man, was too lazy to inflate it, so he put it on the floor and slept on it, uninflated. Perhaps the act of putting it to his lips and inflating it would have been too painful a reminder of his failed conversations with the young lady? That's not for me to say.

As for my buddy's official reason for striking out? Not being a the sort of person to admit to fleeing a woman because she could have been one of the three witches in the myth of Perseus, if, instead of passing around a single eye, they were passing around a single IQ point, my buddy instead came up with a different explanation. An explanation he gave to the shoe salesman was that it was his lack of new shoes that prevented him from having what Bill Clinton would refer to as "relations." I guess his official explanation was as uncredible to the shoe salesman, as it was to me, since my buddy didn't end up getting so much as a coupon for his troubles.

E-Mail From Nigeria

And people wonder why tourists get on my nerves...

Todd Allen

Her Gift In His Lap - A Comedy Of Upset Stomachs

"So, are you two serious," I asked my friend, as he told me about his plans to join a young lady on a boat cruise.

"Will you stop that," he yelled at me. "I'm just going on a cruise. This is not a date."

Clearly, the poor man had a bad case of denial. The young lady in question had met him a couple weeks earlier and was following him around like a lovesick puppy, wide-eyes, tongue hanging out... the real deal. Of course, my friend would hear of no such thing, on the grounds that she was much too young. The poor dear was born after Star Wars was released, after all, and he was almost to the point where he might be approaching middle age. Never mind she was old enough to drink and had even managed to get through college. Like I said, a very bad case of denial.

"So if it's not a date, what are you going along for," I asked, trying to figure out why he was being so naive.

He decided maybe he should see who her friends were and maybe he'd talk to them, because, at least in his mind, he wasn't on a date. When I told him any of her female friends that might happen to be on the boat would have already been told he was off-limits, he got mad again.

Poor deluded man. His protests made his ultimate fate so much worse.

So he went on the boat. He hadn't told me it was the young lady's birthday. It was and she started drinking. Unfortunately, not only could she not hold her liquor very well, but she hadn't eaten, so she had a little trouble standing up. Did I say a little trouble standing up? No, that wouldn't be accurate. Falling down drunk would be a more accurate term.

And so the next phase of their relationship began. Or, as my friend put it, "babysitting."

Yes, even though he didn't think he was on a date, his was the duty of looking after the fallen damsel. Her friends were only too happy to leave them to each other's company. I'm sure he was confused at the time. No, their major contribution was to feed her some cake to try and sober her up. That didn't do any good.

And so, there was my buddy, sitting down, stuck babysitting a young lady so drunk she couldn't stand up. A young lady who'd managed to work her way into his lap.

He looked down and there she was. Lying down with her dizzy head newly resting on his lap. She rocked her head back, gently grinding into his groin, looked up and grinned. The she repeated the grind.

My friend looked down at her and smiled. "Perhaps," he thought to himself. "Perhaps, Todd was correct. Perhaps this girl does like me. Perhaps this evening will have happy ending."

The young lady gazed up at him and smiled.

Uuurrrrrrppppp!!!

Then she threw up all over him.

Todd Allen

He's a nicer guy than I am. He didn't actually try to move her until she stopped puking on him. I would have dumped her on the floor, immediately.

Needless to say, he went home alone, disgusted and dripping wet. He didn't even take solace in how unusual it was to have received such a personalized gift when his wasn't the birthday they were celebrating.

The moral of our story: if they're too drunk to stand up, don't feed them cake.

Perhaps you've heard the theory that a woman is more likely to notice a man if that man is already in the company of another woman (i.e. "he's taken")? The mechanics of this idea, roughly, is that there must be something worthwhile about any man who has a woman in tow... or it's sometimes explained as a function of jealousy. Take your pick, 'cause this week I had a woman giving me the most interested glances, and I thought it was more a case of empathy than the aforementioned theories, or perhaps I should just call it...

The Adventure Of The Sympathetic Waitress

A young lady had decided that since her fiancé didn't want to see the stage version of "The Full Monty," and since I was aware how much bigger her fiancé is than myself, that I would be a safe escort to the theater.

After the show let out, we were hungry, so we lit into a nearby pub, which was just about the only place for a quick burger still open in the area. A strangely nervous manager led us to a table and fumbled with the menus before scurrying off. Presently, a waitress came around. She wasn't as nervous as the manager was, at least not yet, but that's how the fun started.

We ordered our drinks, and the waitress said she'd come take our order when she returned with said drinks. Now my friend was wanting to get back to her fiancé, so she called the waitress back, said that we were in a bit of hurry and were ready to order.

That's when the waitress' attitude changed. Much like the manager had, she started acting a bit nervous when addressing my friend. I didn't think much of it until she came back with our drinks.

When the waitress returned, she glanced nervously at my friend as she set down the first drink. However, when she handed me my Guinness, there was a look of... knowing understanding... on her face. Like she knew the score and felt sorry for me. I was confused, but didn't say anything, knowing full well I'd get a just lecture on imagining that women were looking at me.

The next time the waitress came around, the same thing happened: an apprehensive facial expression when addressing my friend, but a much warmer, even sympathetic expression when looking at me. It was a friendlier glance than the previous.

This was too funny, I thought to myself, and decided to tell my friend, anyway. She was a bit incredulous at the idea, as was to be expected, but sure enough, when the waitress brought the food, the same thing happened. As soon as the waitress was out of earshot, my friend broke out laughing, 'cause she'd finally noticed the same looks I'd been seeing.

I near as I could figure, the waitress had decided we were a couple. It was 10:30 PM and we had theater programs, so I can understand the mistake. But when my friend told the waitress that we were in a hurry, she seemed to have convinced her that she was a bitch on wheels. Naturally, as I am the center of all things kind and innocent in the universe, and probably the most charming man in the place at 10:30 PM on a Thursday night in the Chicago downtown business district, the waitress must have wondered what a nice guy like me was doing with such a pushy broad. And her affection was growing.

E-Mail From Nigeria

The next time around, after the distasteful glance at my friend, I was greeted with a warm smile and something else... the waitress started to slowly wink at me with her left eye. She must've noticed my eyebrow raising, because she quickly blinked her right eye... after the left had closed... to try and cover it up.

I'll be honest with you, this was a cute waitress. I was beginning to think if I was getting this kind of attention because she thought I had a pushy date, maybe my friend should throw a screaming fit and storm out of the pub when she finished eating. I figured if I walked over to the bar, acted somewhat remorseful and ordered a beer, I'd probably get all the attention I could handle. My friend actually thought it was a good idea and that I'd get more than just sympathy. You figure if a woman tells me that... Unfortunately, it was 11:30 PM and I had a sports column that needed editing before the morning.

Still, while this was a bit more extreme, it's not the first time I've suddenly gotten attention while dining with a woman. I've a couple (married) female friends I occasionally have lunch with, and I frequently get similar, if more subdued, reactions. There may be something to this particular theory of attraction. All I know is, one of these days, I'm going to be out with a female friend and not have something that needs doing before the morning, and the next time it happens, that friend _will_ be throwing a fit, and we're going to see how this business of women being attracted to men they perceive as "taken" really works.

Todd Allen

Propositioned - In Front Of Her Brothers

It's a nice feeling to be wanted. Unfortunately, sometimes being wanted can get you into all kinds of trouble.

It was nearing midnight as I sauntered into an Irish bar, wandered to the back, and ordered a pint of Guinness, as I am wont to do. Taking a sip, I strolled towards the front of the bar to have a look at the clientele. I wasn't two sips into my drink before a young blonde woman approached me and, in a thick Irish accent, demanded to borrow my glasses.

I get this every now and again, usually from someone in a bachelorette party, so I complied and handed over my glasses. Predictably, she was a little freaked out by the strength of my lenses and led me over to show her friends, not all of whom were female, and none of whom appeared to be getting married.

Upon returning my glasses, she swore up and down that she knew me. I inquired as to how we knew each other and she said we'd been dancing in that bar. Ask anyone that knows me, I don't dance. I used to drink with some professional dancers, and they assured me that my closest attempts do not qualify as actual dancing. Suffice it to say, I'm not just white, my ancestry is partially English, so I'm much too stiff to dance.

Not being completely clueless, and realizing this was not a bachelorette I was dealing with, after all, it was pretty obvious when she was asking me to "dance," she wasn't asking about the kind of dancing that evolves music, and she demonstrated her euphemism with her hips and a nod of the head.

Like I said, it's a nice feeling to be wanted, but it can create some problems. First, the young lady was already motioning in the general direction of the door and I had all but two sips of my pint left. I simply do not like to waste a perfectly good pint of Guinness. It's bad karma. Then there was the slight matter of the group of people she was with. Two other young women and five men. I realized she was with these men, but she wasn't flirting with any of them and they weren't flirting with her... and they were looking at me awfully funny. As I took a sip of my drink to stall for time and try to get a little better picture of what was going on, I noticed the slightly grimacing men had Irish accents, and then it dawned on me: these men were her brothers.

I'm not sure how such things work in Ireland, but where I grew up, it just wasn't a good idea to be talking about slipping out for a little nookie with a girl in front of her brothers, and it really didn't matter who initiated the conversation. I was starting to get the impression that was a universal custom, and I took note of how much bigger than I, these 5 guys were. Let's just say it would have been imprudent for me to ask them if they thought Notre Dame's "Fighting Irish" team mascot was an unfair representation of Irish culture, 'cause if they were the fighting kind of Irish, there wasn't any chance I'd be able to avoid the hospital if all five of them decided they didn't like me. Personally, I like to avoid hospitals.

Then I got to thinking, if I turned down their sister, they might get upset that I thought their sister wasn't good enough for me, and they might beat me, anyway.

So there I was caught between two excuses for some protective-looking brothers to beat me to a bloody pulp.

I only had one out: I played dumb. I mean I played naïve, stupid and alcoholic.

"I can't dance yet," I said. "I just got my first beer. It's a Saturday night and a man needs to do some drinking. Y'know?"

At this point both her and her brothers looked confused. Still, the brothers were looking the annoyed part of confused, as I was still turning her down. So I backed up and introduced myself, and asked her name. This threw everybody for loop. When she got done introducing herself, she again wanted to "dance," but I reverted to my need to have a couple drinks before I could contemplate any non-drinking activity, and that I was a terrible dancer. She suggested that perhaps we could do something later, and shuffled off, half bewildered, wondering how I could have thought she was really talking about dancing.

I retreated to the back of the bar, and I hoped the act worked. It mostly did. One of the brothers did try and trip me, but I wasn't nearly as drunk as he thought I was, and I managed to get my foot untangled with his, so I merely stumbled, instead of falling on my face, but not enough to spill my drink. The other four just seemed to feel sorry that someone could be as oblivious as I pretended to be and seemed to have a quick word with him, once I'd gotten away. They didn't bother me after that.

Was I wrong about Irish brothers being over-protective? Who's to say, but I do know this: the young lady was certainly doing her share of flirting, with her brother always looming in the background, and she never did leave the bar while I was there. Given her extraordinary initiative, I wonder whose fault that was?

Mental note: in the future, avoid women with male siblings.

E-Mail From Nigeria

Behind The Orange Curtain

Or

The Naïve And Sentimental Patron

I was having a drink at one of my local haunts, when I happened across a promotional party. Liquor distributors often pay a couple good-looking women to visit various bars and hand out samples of products and some branded give-away items. Tonight was no exception, except this time it wasn't the fellow dressed up like the Captain Morgan pirate running around with two scantily clad assistants. This time, it was two young lovelies pushing a liqueur that for the purposes of this account shall be called "Couture." (Names have been changed to protect the guilty, as usual.)

Towards the front of the bar, the Couture Girls had set up a little display. In front, on a table, they had a bottle of their booze, a martini shaker, (to mix their samples) and a tray with little plastic shot glasses. That's all standard issue for the biz.

Behind that table, was something unusual: a set of orange curtains. The Couture Girls had brought in their own curtains, which they'd leaned up against the wall and had more or less created a de facto booth. From where I was sitting at the end of the bar, I could see about half of the booth's interior, between the curtain and the Golden Tee video game they set up next to. I could tell they had something in the booth, limes to mix with their product, for one thing, but my view of the edge was obscured. Still, it's important to note that the side of the booth was open.

Presently, it was announced that the Couture Girls had some prizes behind those orange curtains, so I sauntered over to the general area. Three guys were getting free shots, er, samples and were also being given gifts. In this case, little orange pouches you could strap around your wrist and wear like I watch. No, I didn't understand those either. I approached Couture Girl #1 and said, "So what's behind the curtain... besides limes?"

Couture Girl #1 smiled, walked over to Couture Girl #2, and whispered something in her ear. The two of them got rid of the guys they were giving the samples to. Then Couture Girl #2, the more attractive of the two, as luck would have it, beckoned me into booth.

Once inside, she said "just a minute," and proceeded to untie and close the curtains behind her.

"Now we're alone," she said and stepped in front of me.

She leaned her face forward until was six inches in front of mine and said, in a breathy voice, "Tell me something Couture-versial about yourself," pronouncing Couture-versial as close to controversial as she could while still vamping.

"It's OK, I won't tell anyone," she finished.

It was kind of a strange situation to be in. Liquor promotion girls are usually a bunch of big flirts, but this was a little over the top for flirting and she'd shut the curtain, which was also odd. I literally wasn't sure if I was being propositioned or not. Then I remembered you could see through the side of the booth and that my friend, the manager... the female manager... was standing about where I was when I first peered into the booth from afar, and she was bound to flip out and start screaming if she saw me extending too much affection to someone working a promotion.

"I published a book called 'Beware the Club Girls,'" I said, deciding to air on the side of caution.

"Cool," she said, smiled, and offered me a choice between a hat and a visor, definitely better fare than the silly wrist-pouches she'd given out earlier.

I put the hat on and turned to exit the booth, supposing that since her behavior was significantly less forward that the mood had passed her.

"What's your name," she asked. "I want to look up your book."

I gave her my card, figuring it was the "Couture" thing to do.

The rest of the promotion passed without incident, and after they left at midnight, I asked some of my friends who'd been sitting next to the "booth" how many people had been asked behind the curtain. To my horror, I was the only one who'd had the curtain closed for privacy, and I'd effectively blown her off. One of my friends was somewhat upset, as I'd told him about the incident and he'd even come up with a line to use on Couture Girl #2, should an offer be directed towards him.

Oh, I can be such a naïve fool. I think I screwed up.

Todd Allen

Hate Mail From A Spring Break College Girl Gone Wild

Ever get hate mail from a woman? It's happened to me on occasion.

Last week I got an e-mail from a young lady I'd met in a nightclub the night before. Have a look at it yourself, knowing that the name (*) has been changed to protect the guilty.

so like, were we totally there just to amuse you or what? it was like so fun and stuff. but this like semi-twisted life that you live vicariously through (and at the expense of) other people really makes me question, do i really want to move to such a welcoming environment as chicago. for real, i just gotta say that it is so funny how both karma and myself can be a real bitch.

("Muffy"*)

and one more thing, should i send my hospital bill directly to you or care of indignant.com

And you might wonder what it was that I did to this young lady. I wonder, too.

The evening I met the young lady (we'll assume she qualifies for the term lady), I had been to a business reception and accompanied some friends to a nightclub, once the reception ended. One member of the group came back to the area we were sitting with four young ladies, put his arm around one of them and somehow managed to survive a few hours without so much as coming up for air, if you follow me. Of the remaining 3 young ladies, two of

E-Mail From Nigeria

them really didn't say that much, and the fourth proceeded to start job prospecting the men in my entourage. After she figured out there probably wasn't a job to be had, the fourth, who seemed more articulate than her friends (and, as stereotypes would have, was the token non-blonde in the group), started talking to me.

It would seem that the four young lovelies were on Spring Break from Central Michigan University. Why anyone would come to Chicago for Spring Break is beyond me, but that's why they were in front of me. Well, that and the waitress at Hooters recommended the club to them, or so I was told.

The fourth young lovely, we'll call her "Muffy," seemed nice enough, a bit cocky, but being 21 and cute will do that. She later admitted she hadn't been using her real name, rather, her and her three friends were using the names they would choose for their first born. Yeah, I thought that was a little weird, too. Kinda like when I had a college girlfriend start reading Bride Magazine after we'd been going out for a couple days. Maybe it's a college thing?

I had a pleasant enough chat with her, then she got up and decided she wanted to dance with another member of the group I'd walked in with. The four young lovelies seemed to pair off with four young men (I'd hesitate to characterize them as a collection of studs, but they did have jobs) and everybody decided to leave. I figured there wasn't a whole lot of sense in chasing after a 21-year-old whose friends had already paired up at 3am, especially when I had business to take care of in the morning.

Sure enough, I got that e-mail the following evening. Looking back, I never so much as bought Muffy a drink, and I left separately. So it's a mystery to me what she's talking about. I can't figure out for the life of me how I rate hate mail when I didn't even dance with her (although

Todd Allen

I'm told I'm such a bad dancer that if I had danced with her, it might be a legitimate reason).

So, Muffy, my little Spring Break College Girl Gone Wild, wherever you are, since you got such a charge watching me live vicariously at the expense of others (which I guess means having a drink and not pawing at your group), this week's column is for you. After all, who am I to deny audience expectations (and pass up some material that's too bizarre for me to make up)? And when I occasionally refer to meeting a disproportionate number of addled women, you, Muffy, shall be at the vanguard of examples.

And one more thing, that's IndignantOnline.com, not Indignant.com.

E-Mail From Nigeria

The Virgin Of Evanston Affair

"Its 2 AM, do you think he's home or at her place," giggled my friend as she swigged her beer.

"Why don't you call him and find out," suggested my friend's incrementally more sober husband.

"An excellent idea," I agreed and weaved over to the bar's phone booth.

Ring. Ring.

"Hello?" Stan answered. Apparently he'd made it home.

"How was your big date," I inquired.

"I don't want to talk about it," Stan replied with the weariness that only a truly awful date can bring to a voice.

My buddy Stan (or so we'll call him in this tale, for he blushes too much in real life for me to add to his shades of crimson) had not been having a lot of luck with the lovely ladies of Chicago. Indeed, since moving here, his experiences had been one disaster after another, including, but not limited to, the time his date asked the waitress when she was due and the waitress wasn't pregnant. We're talking excruciatingly bad dates, here.

About a month prior to that scene, I had just gotten back from a trip to NYC that included a 40-hour flight delay on the way home. As I was watching 150 e-mails download, there was a knock at the door. It was Stan, and he was on a mission.

"We're going to this charity ball fundraiser thing tonight," he ejaculated.

"Why would I want to do that, and aren't you a little under-dressed for a ball," I asked. I hadn't had a great deal of sleep in the last three days, not that I spent much of it at LaGuardia… I'd been in Mid-Town Manhattan most of the time and refused to set foot in the airport until I had a guaranteed seat on a flight, none of this stand-by crap, but I'd had 2 flights cancelled on me in 8 – 10 hour intervals. I craved my pillow and wasn't up for formalities. And then there was Stan's attire. Slacks and a 70s-esque shirt with three buttons open, attempting to show off a gold chain and a chest that looked like it had been attacked by Rogaine.

I looked up Stan's ball, and it turned out it was a black tie affair and since neither of us was dressed for it, especially Stan, I managed to get out of going. I asked him why he was so dead set on going to that ball, and he told me a strange story.

Earlier that evening, he'd been out jogging with a young lady whom he'd been hanging out with of late. Since they'd gone somewhere each of the two preceding weekends, he asked her what she was doing on Saturday. The young lady waited to answer until they'd reached a corner and there were a few people around. She then proceeded to scream "I'm not interested in you," at Stan. Rude woman, I'd say. Since she'd been planning on attending the charity function in question, Stan had a mind to attend and show her up. I told him I'd find another charity event the next Friday, and we'd go find him a nice society girl then.

Next Friday arrived and there was only one charity event available: a wig-themed event for Mount Sinai hospital. I figured if they were doing a wig motif, I might as well have some fun, so I put on an outfit that vaguely fell into the category of 70s pimp and had half of a small wig hanging out of my shirt. I grabbed Stan and we went to said event. Upon entering I quickly learned two things:

1) Mount Sinai is a Jewish hospital, and tended to have its fundraisers attended by young ladies that adhere, dare I say cling to, the stereotype of the Jewish American Princess.

2) Such young ladies have very little by way of sense of humor.

Now the Jewish thing wasn't really a problem, especially since Stan is Jewish on his mother's side. He actually thought it was funny I didn't realize what kind of a party we were going to. The sense of humor thing was a bit of a problem though. I was getting looked down the nose at... severely, and while Stan was well dressed, he wasn't "club" dressed and the blank looks that accompany the triumph of style over substance were going in every direction but ours. Actually, there was another problem. The open bar we paid a cover charge for didn't include anything I cared to drink so I had to pay for something decent over and above everything else. Bad form.

Eventually a couple of young ladies decided that my costume had more personality than the rest of the people there. I quickly steered them right into Stan. He hit it off with one of them, so I directed him upstairs, where it was quieter and they had some couches to lounge on. I even tried to talk up the young lady's friend to give Stan a chance for some "quality time," and to get the ever-elusive phone number.

Talking up the young lady's friend was not as easy as one might think. This girl was dense. I mean, I was consciously trying to eliminate words of over two syllables from my vocabulary during the conversation, and since there was absolutely nothing we had in common, all I could really do was comment on places I'd eaten in Evanston, the suburb she was from. I could have had a more intelligent conversation with a box of rocks that had been bleached to have any extra intelligence removed from them. I did this for 45 minutes, and was convinced that if Stan didn't get somewhere in the time that I was suffering, I was going to take him out and beat him.

Stan did get a phone number and they went out a couple times. It seemed that she was a 30-year-old single schoolteacher from Evanston, and was possibly a bit on the clingy side. They seemed to like each other, and for the third date, she wanted him to come up to Evanston and visit her.

Knowing that I'd gone to college in Evanston, Stan asked some advice where to eat. Not a problem. When pontificating on food rations, it came out that Stan thought something was up with the young lady, when she invited him to her lair, so to speak.

That is how I came to be in a bar with two other mutual friends of Stan, wondering exactly where the naughty boy was at 2AM and what he was doing.

Eventually, the truth of the matter did come out.

The evening had started off quite well. They had a lovely dinner, and went to the beach afterwards. She'd brought a blanket, which they laid out and started to get cozy. It was then that the young lady decided she wanted to give it up to Stan. You know, as Shakespeare wrote in Othello, to "make the beast with two backs." Now normally, this is not something that would be upsetting to Stan, especially as she was a cute little thing. But alas, this was not a normal situation. The young lady, in phrasing her intentions, had explained to Stan that she was, in fact, a 30-year-old virgin.

Oh, I would pay money to see the look on Stan's face when that popped out.

E-Mail From Nigeria

As Stan explained it to me, on top of the improbability of an attractive 30-year-old woman still being a virgin, there were certain cultural issues factoring into his shock. First off, Stan is a gentleman and probably wouldn't deflower someone on the third date. He's not *that* forward. Secondly, Stan figured that if she was a 30-year-old Jewish virgin schoolteacher, getting jiggy with her would lead directly, unequivocally, to marriage, possibly involving a shotgun, regardless of whether or not she was in the family way. Apparently, he'd met the type before, and that was a de facto marriage proposal he'd been given. At any rate, as a gentleman, and as a man not yet ready for matrimony... at least not on the third date, Stan did the only thing he could do:

"Look at the time," Stan said as he casually glanced at his watch. "I have to be getting home."

Now there was a problem getting home. Stan had taken the train to Evanston, and the Evanston train stopped running at midnight. It was 12:20 AM. Being a gentleman, Stan really couldn't bring himself to have her drive him all the way back downtown where lived. Especially since he knew he wasn't going to be seeing her again. He decided the gentlemanly thing to do would be to have her drop him off at the Howard train station.

Perhaps I should explain what the corner by the Howard train station is like. Ever see "Boyz in the Hood?" Imagine a little patch of gang-ridden South Central L.A. transplanted to Chicago. That's what Stan got out of the car and walked through. Just to complete his evening, the train track was under construction closer to downtown, and the connecting bus they put him on got stuck in a traffic jam behind an accident.

We suspect Stan is subconsciously attempted to set a record for most frustrating date. I do know this: I'm not introducing him to any more women. I don't want to be blamed for the next date.

Todd Allen

An Over-Stimulated Drunk Woman Broke My Glasses

I got home Saturday night, or was it Sunday morning? At that time of the night, the day of the week is a subjective thing. I was tired and I had precious little time to sleep before I was supposed to be somewhere else. I prepared my self for bed, sat down, and took off my glasses. Except, taking off my glasses didn't quit go as it should have.

Part of my frames were still resting on my right ear, while the rest of my glasses were in my hand. This puzzled me, somewhat. I reached to my ear and found the wire that wraps behind my ear was, indeed still behind my ear, while the right arm of the frames had been severed about half an inch in front of my ear, yet both pieces of my glasses had remained on my head the entire evening.

At that point I decided I wanted to go to bed and not deal with it until the morning.

You might wonder what it would take to break a pair of glasses, while a man was wearing them, in such a way that he didn't notice it happening. It didn't take me that long to figure out, as there was only one thing it could have been:

I had walked into my friends' bar and ordered a drink. In short order, I was approached by a young lady whom I knew in passing. She'd had a couple drinks and was a little, shall we say, full of life. She also felt like being the good Samaritan... I guess. I was told that she really wanted to help me with my hair. I occasionally get this from women, now that I've grown my hair out, and it usually means they want to play with my hair. I know, it's a rough life, but somebody has to be an object of amusement. Sure enough, she babbled on about how she couldn't make up her mind what suited me best, and she started tugging on my hair fairly hard. Now I understand some women do like to have their hair pulled, but this guy doesn't, so I started trying to remove myself from the rapidly sinking situation. As near as I can tell, she must have grabbed the arm of my frame right about at the point I'd twisted it a couple years back, where it was weakened and yanked on it while she was pulling my hair. Since she was alternating yanking and patting the hair down, trying to find her personal aesthetic for my hair, she must've tucked the earpiece back in place, and the frames were a custom fit, so they still stayed in place with only an arm and a half. I had no clue something was wrong until I took them off.

To add insult to injury, she thought I should look to Paul Ruebens for hair style inspiration. Apparently Pee Wee spikes his hair now? All I know is it cost me $15 bucks to get my frames laser-soldered back together, and that a drunk woman broke my glasses while playing with my hair. I'm afraid what else she might break if she's in a better mood. I think I'll maintain a safe distance next time, 'cause I hate hospitals.

Todd Allen

My New Definition Of A Hook-Up Bar

I have a new definition of the term "hook-up bar." Literally, I have been to a place that sets the new standard, by which all other bars shall be judged, and it's not merely the clientele establishing this standard. No, the bartenders are among the most helpful I've ever encountered.

So, I walk in the door and call a friend of mine, who'd wanted to know how a prank I was playing had progressed. She answers the phone, asks if I want to go see a band and tells me to go to my building's lobby immediately. Sure enough, two minutes later I'm sandwiched in the back seat, next to the husband of the band's lead singer, which was a little awkward, as the band's lead singer had spent half an hour rummaging around inside my mouth, the week before. OK, so she was cleaning my teeth at the dentist's office, rock diva's have day jobs, too.

Anyway, I find out we're going to a bar on the South Side of Chicago. I've heard of this bar, and usually I hear about it in the context of it being one of Jenny McCarthy's old neighborhood hangouts, which is not exactly dampening my enthusiasm for the trip.

We get there and two things stand out about the place: the patrons are young and as homogenous as all get out.

One of the people I went with used to own a bar. After a bit, he said there was something bothering him. I pointed at a very petite young blonde thing and asked if her looking like she was 16 was bothering him.

"Oh that's it," he said. "They're not carding. OK, that's cool."

Now I'm not saying they weren't carding, all I'm saying is the patrons looked real young. College young. First couple of years of college young. And a couple of them looked like they should leave early 'cause it was a school night. Fortunately, I know that nobody on the South Side of Chicago would ever dream of participating in underage drinking. Absolutely not.

That really wasn't a factor in this being my new definition of a hook-up bar. The homogenous make-up of the crowd, however was. Looking around, I would have thought 80% of the crowd were blood relatives. Similar facial features. Give or take a few pounds, similar builds. There were numerous clusters of young ladies that were obviously sisters, and who looked about 8 months apart in age. I was noticing when a group of young ladies would walk in, they would be wearing extremely similar outfits (two in sleeveless shirts and leather pants, a quartet that looked like they left a volley ball game, the tie-dyed group, etc.) and a few sets of young ladies were wearing the exact same outfit. I particularly remember a pair of girls wearing the exact same gray top and black pants. The top was the sort of shirt that plays peek-a-boo with the mid-riff any time the wearer moves. Thing is, there was a 15 pound difference between the two ladies and the exposed mid-riff of one was more appropriate than on the other, if you follow me. Exact same outfit though.

One of the women I was there with mentioned the guys there had the exact same trends going. It's like I stepped into a different country. Still, because everyone looks so much alike, really the only difference between them is the clothing they're wearing. By achieving that level of homogeny, the bar has rendered the point of which partner you leave with relatively moot. They all look the same. No one is significantly better looking. No pressure to find the pick of the litter, no worries that your friend will have a better catch than you. In short, there's a lot of B.S. that just goes straight out the window. If you don't hit it off with the first person you talk to, just move on the next. There's no difference. And that's what everyone seemed to be doing. Heck, personality might actually count, there. I've never seen anything like it.

The homogeny factor is a component of why this place is my new definition of a hook-up bar, but what really put it over the top was the experienced and friendly bar staff. They really seemed dedicated to helping their customers hook-up. Pimp-daddies with a beer tap, if you will. How do they do it? I was standing at the bar, ordering a pint of Guinness, as I am wont to do. Two chairs over, with a pile of coats between us, was one of the women I'd come to the bar with. Independently of me, she ordered a drink. I didn't say anything to bartender about her; she didn't say anything about me. Next thing I know, he's handing a drink to both of us and I'm getting the bill for both. Yup, that's right, I guess if you're a guy and your standing next to a gal, the bartender will go the extra mile and help you buy her a drink, breaking the ice and all. Think about it, if all the ladies are the same level of cute, buying one a drink is pretty much the same as buying another lady a drink. Unfortunately, the young lady in question was there with her fiancé. I told him about it, figuring it was less likely I'd get my ass kicked if he heard it from me and not her. This was the former bar owner. He chuckled and said it was probably good for business. I wasn't sure if he meant cash business or monkey business.

Still, I've never seen a bar so dedicated to hooking people up. Ladies and gentleman, the new standard for a hook-up bar has been established.

E-Mail From Nigeria

The Adventure of the Middle-Aged Make-Out Table

You know what I love about New York? If I decide to go out and have an adventure on a Saturday night, I don't have to go looking for the adventure, it comes looking for me.

I walked into an Irish pub down by the Southern border of Murray Hill and the band hadn't started playing. The stools at the bar were all occupied, and being one to sit down when I drink, I wandered back and found the only empty space in the joint. I sat down at the table and sipped at my Guinness as I tried to decide who I was going to talk into filling the empty chair across the table from me.

That decision was not fated to be in my sphere of control.

A rather noisy group came in, and started commiserating by the edge of the bar near my table. Among this group were some likely candidates for my empty chair. Indeed, one member of that group was as attractive a young lady as recent memory can conjure up.

That's when the PDA started. I'm not talking Personal Digital Assistant. No, I'm talking about the old fashioned hormones rushing, hands wandering, openings probed Public Display of Affection.

A man in his early 50s staggered in, his belly looking like it was ready to pop out triplets at any second. He grabbed a woman in her early 40s, who unlike this fellow, was fit and immaculately groomed, and put her in an aggressive lip lock. They clinched long enough that they must have been practicing what trumpet players called circular breathing, and staggered backwards, still entwined with each other until they landed in the empty chair across the table from me. And that's when it really started to heat up. The drunk guy was grabbing at her thighs and she was climbing over his lap as they continued to attempt a mutual tonsillectomy. Talk about aiming for home plate.

I sat there, slightly taken aback. I wasn't sure what the polite response for an uninvited snogging session usurping your table was, but there weren't any other empty seats and I damn well wasn't giving mine up.

After a bit, perhaps due to lack of oxygen, they stopped. The woman detached herself and returned to her friends. The fellow turned to me, saw what was, no doubt, a puzzled look on my face and apologized for taking my seat.

"It's alright," I told him. "I understand urges." And in a sense, I suppose it's comforting to see evidence that your sex drive doesn't disappear at the first sight of middle age. I was about to have him bring over that particularly attractive young lady with his party, when the poor man passed out. Too much excitement, I suppose.

And there I was, once again, sitting at my table and looking confusedly at the spectacle before me.

Eventually, the fellow's little friend came over to see what was going on. She brought a couple of her friends with her, including the one I'd been hoping would come over, so at least part of my makeshift plan was working. I glanced at the passed out man, shrugging my shoulders, and the young lovely started to approach me. It was too good a plan to work, and, sure enough, another of the group seemed to think I must be a weirdo to be sitting at that table and pulled her back. As if I was the one initiating anything.

After a lot of chuckling, it was decided the sleeping giant should be awakened. Did they tap him on the shoulder? No, that would be civilized. Instead, his female companion turned around, leaned her backside into his lap and started to do a grind like she was dancing for dollars. Sure enough, he woke up in a good mood and they started making out again. As soon as they stopped making out, he went back to sleep.

By the time this cycle had repeated itself twice more, and it did, I had finished my Guinness and started contemplating my options. I wanted another drink, but if I got up, I wasn't going to have a seat when I got back and the amorous antics at the other end of the "Middle-Aged Make-Out Table" were certainly keeping the rest of the women in the place away from me, so I decided to seek my next beverage at a different pub.

Still, if you measure life in the value of anecdotes and how many new things you see, you'd have to call the evening a success. Lord knows I'd never seen a horny narcoleptic in action before. As a certain gossip columnist is wont to say, "Only in New York."

Todd Allen

E-Mail From Nigeria

Travel

Todd Allen

E-Mail From Nigeria

Trapped In Flight Delay Hell

There must be some sort of cosmic law that I'm denied the luxury of hassle-free travel. The last time I'd snuck out to New York City for a job interview, my flight home was twice-delayed for a total of 40 hours of waiting and I had to come up with some pretty creative explanations for my prolonged absence from work. The trip before that, I missed my flight because someone on the train I took to the airport had a seizure and they stopped the train.

This past week, the infamous Mr. Cussy persuaded me to attend a costume party in Miami. "Take Ghost Airlines," he said, telling me their fares were low and that his friend, whose place I would be crashing at (never mind this guy threw me out of the house, last time I was in town), said it would be fine. Cussy lied to me.

Unlike previous trips, there were no problems taking the train to the airport. Once I got to the airport, for reasons that escape my tenuous grasp of logic, I discovered my domestic flight left from the international terminal. After a twenty-five minute walk to Terminal 5 (normally, you just take a cab directly to the international terminal... if you know that's where you're going), I found not only was I required to check-in at the front desk, never mind they'd already mailed me the tickets, but the check-in line was 30 people deep with 25 minutes until the departure time. As a few annoyed travelers around me discussed the dismal prospects of everyone getting checked in before the plane took off, we got the word that said flight was to be delayed 90 minutes.

It seems some unfortunate passenger had a mid-air heart attack and forced an emergency landing in Chattanooga.

A situation eerily similar to the epileptic seizure-induced train delay that made me miss my flight to New Orleans. Isn't it awful having themes in your life?

Bad omens continued, as it turned out the flight was departing from the furthest gate in the terminal and the first moving walkway wasn't moving. Ever get the feeling you should just cut your losses and head home? I must be a glutton for punishment. I kept walking towards the departure gate.

As I got to the gate, for the fourth time since my arrival, I heard the public service announcement, "Baggage left unattended will be picked up by the Chicago Police Department." It occurred to me that if Cussy brought a couple of his deranged ex-girlfriends to the airport, perhaps the CPD would remove his unwanted baggage.

Because the flight was so late, it seems that the departure gate had moved over by one gate, so all the would-be passengers sitting at the original gate (roughly a quarter of them already sacked out) were asked to get up and move, seeing as how Ghost no longer had possession of the gate. It got funnier when the gate's new owner showed up, a mystery plane with "Air Plus" as it's markings that landed and received attention from the ground crew... but nobody departed the plane. No airline staff was at the gate. No flight arrival information was posted. Our own flight's people had no idea where the plane came from or what an "Air Plus" was. Yup, a genuine encounter with a phantom aircraft and all that was missing were some men in black suits. Well... technically speaking, I was wearing a black suit. Never mind.

When we finally did board the plane, I found myself in the back row of the plane and directly in front of the toilet, cursing the check-in wench, of whom I'd told I didn't have a preference of window or aisle, I just didn't want the rear of the plane. Of course, she must've hated the guy sitting next to me even more. She had him sitting one row behind me, which would have placed him on the toilet for the duration of the flight. Another fellow was assigned a seat two rows behind me, which, near as I could tell, would have him seated on top of the emergency exit.

After boarding, we sat and waited. After around half an hour, the pilot announced he had some paperwork, related to the sick passenger and emergency landing, which he had to finish filling out before we could take off. Half an hour later, that being a full hour after the plane boarded, we started to move. Not taking off, mind you, just moving. It was another 20 minutes before we were actually in the air. Roughly speaking, a 2 hour and 45 minute delay on a 2 hour and 55 minute flight. I'm so glad the pilot couldn't fill out the paperwork sometime when a plane full of people weren't strapped in. I wouldn't want anything reasonable to happen when I travel.

As for the flight itself, it was noisy as hell. My seat was on the wing and, by proxy, by the engine. Ever watch a movie about a World War II bombing mission? Remember that loud, annoying engine noise you hear while the bomber's in flight? That's pretty much what I was hearing for the whole flight. Probably should have brought earplugs.

Remember how I was seated by the toilet? Well, of the two bathrooms in the aft section, one was apparently out of service, so most of a flight, there's a pile-up of people waiting to answer nature's call clogging up the aisle right next to my seat.

And since this flight left at the dinner hour (technically speaking boarded prior to and took off during the dinner hour), you might ask what was for supper? Cheddar-flavored crackers. And I loathe cheddar-flavored crackers. What ever happened to peanuts on airplanes?

Just to make my flight complete, as the plane is landing, I get hit with a splash of water. Being a little disturbed that

Todd Allen

I'm getting splashed, I asked the flight attendant where the water came from. Eventually, he was able to trace it to a small leak in the rook of the cabin. Only in luxury class do you get a shower with your flight. I mean really, how did I rate this 5-star service?

So my flight is three hours late arriving. All-in-all, this wasn't the most horrible thing ever to happen to me, as Cussy's flight was originally arriving three hours after mine. I'd planned on hopping a cab to a movie theater before returning to the airport, but this way, I figured his flight should be arriving at almost the same time I was, so we could immediately grab the rental car and proceed to South Beach to pursue super-models.

I looked at the arrival board and saw Cussy's flight was listed as on-time. I turned around and saw his arrival gate was right behind me, but no plane was there, which was strange, 'cause if the plane was really on time, it should have arrived 10 minutes prior. I parked myself for another 10 minutes and was about to go looking for an airline rep. when someone yelled to his girlfriend, "It's not getting in until 11:30."

Wonderful. Cussy's plane also had a two and a half hour delay. That made over five hours of plane delays to plague me in one day. It also didn't quite leave me enough time to catch a movie. Worse, we had 11:30 dinner reservations, and I was supposed to be introduced to a Dolphins cheerleader. You just don't deprive a man of personal introductions to professional cheerleaders. It's wrong.

So I tried to kill two hours in the airport. Unfortunately, I'd flown into Fort Lauderdale, instead of Miami International, which is probably the equivalent of flying into Midway instead of O'Hare. The place was shut down. I couldn't even get proper food. The only thing open in the terminal I was at was a snack shop that charged me $5 and change for a Coke and a chocolate chip cookie and the next terminal over was just as dead. I ended up going into the bathroom and shaving, inadvertently freaking out a couple passers-by who probably thought I was some sort of criminal on the run. Not that I remotely cared at that point.

How late was Cussy's flight? They shut down the damn terminal before it arrived. Everyone was kicked out, and anybody waiting for a delayed flight had to wait near the exit.

So you're thinking Cussy's flight got in, we grabbed a car, sped to South Beach and started swimming in supermodels. Anyone else would have, but not when I'm traveling. No, that would be too easy.

Cussy's flight arrived about 11:30, just like they said. Never mind they were apparently either too embarrassed or too lazy to update any of the arrival monitors at the airport. Then again, at least three people commented to me that Ghost is chronically late into and out of Fort Lauderdale. The fellow whose pad I was crashing at told me he had a 7 hour flight delay the one and only time he flew them and that he most assuredly never endorsed the airline to Cussy. I never did find out why Cussy's flight was delayed, but at least on his flight, they had free cocktails to compensate for the delay. All my cheapskate flight crew coughed up was a tumbler of ginger ale and a bag of cheddar-flavored crackers.

So Cussy arrives. He's less than thrilled to see me, as I'm holding up a sign with a rather guttural Hindi slang term for homosexual on it and pointing at him, just like a limo driver. Not only did the two Indian women he'd been hitting on see it, but their mother did too. Too bad, but I was more interested in that cheerleader. Cussy tells me he's switched our dinner reservations to 1am, when the Blue Door's kitchen closes. After waiting around for his luggage to come around, we set off to find the rental car. Eventually, a bus came to take us to the rental agent and we waited through a long-enough line for that time of night. Then yet another problem cropped up.

Cussy was very particular about the car he wanted. He wanted a Jaguar. Specifically, he wanted a Jaguar S-Type. Not just any old Jaguar would do, you see, for Cussy has an image to maintain and if it's not couture, it's just not happening. I'd been hearing, for at least 2 weeks, about how he'd gotten confirmation on an S-Type. Well, there was a little problem. Apparently whoever the genius that took his order was, he didn't put down the model preference, and the rental guys didn't want to give us an S-Type, they wanted to give us an XJ8. Now, while you and I might think that a Jaguar is Jaguar, Cussy will be the first to inform you that this simply is not the case. Believe me, as I heard him explain it to the rental agent about five times, as the realization started to set in that I wasn't eating at the Blue Door and I wasn't getting a personal introduction to a Dolphin's cheerleader.

The aggravating thing was that they had an S-Type in front of the building and they just didn't want to give it to us. That would change, but at 1 am, dinner reservations now unavoidably missed, I convinced Cussy we should just take the bloody XJ8 while the bars were still open. He agreed, but informed the rental agent we would be back the next day and they'd damn well better have an S-Type when we returned.

You might think this was end of my traveling problems. Again, you'd be wrong.

As we entered South Beach, we turned down the radio, only to hear the squeaking of our brake pads. Lovely. Just what I wanted. Be stuck with the bill for a $60,000 car because they gave me one with no breaks. Oh well, I thought to myself, Cussy signed for the car, and as long as I didn't get killed in the crash, the condition of the car really wasn't my problem.

E-Mail From Nigeria

We lucked out and the brakes held out long enough to park. Cussy called the rental twits as we chowed down at the News Café and amazingly avoided stuttering when a group of semi-clothed partygoers passed our sidewalk table. He told them we were going to be returning the car, as we liked to be able to stop when there were things in front of us, and that they'd better have an S-Type for us.

10 minutes later, they called back. They did have an S-Type for us. Mr. Shariq told them we'd be in around 5 am to pick it up.

We finished eating, inadvertently chased Keanu Reeves out of a club, and returned the car at 5 am. Son of bitch, if they weren't ready to sign over the very same S-Type they said we couldn't have a scant 4 hours earlier. Well, actually, the agent didn't really want to sign it over until his manager returned at 7am, but we played a little good customer, bad customer and he relented. I don't think he wanted us lurking about for two hours and we were just about annoyed enough to stick around.

Like I said, I have the worst transportation problems when I travel.

My flight home wasn't quite as bad. The flight boarded on time. Then we waited 25 minutes for somebody to duct tape a tray that wouldn't stay up. After all, if a tray isn't locked in upright position, the distribution of its weight will cause the airplane to go into a tailspin. Really. It's a safety precaution we mustn't take lightly. Definitely worth wasting half an hour of my life.

And yes, I took a cab home.

Todd Allen

Breaking Down Racial Stereotypes... With A Radiation Suit

If you've never been to Miami Beach, you have to understand that a fair amount of the culture is about showing off. Ocean Drive is as much about being seen as it is about staring at the spandex. People show off their bodies, clothes, children and dogs. Most of time you don't really mind the pretty people and the spandex outfits they're almost wearing. I was, however, extremely disturbed by the lady who was parading her daughter around in a stroller. The daughter, a homely creature, was maybe two years old, probably younger and not only had earrings, but was wearing lipstick. Can you imagine being so embarrassed your kid's ugly that you have her in make up while she's still in the stroller? Sad thing was, the kid was still hard on the eyes. This sort of thing doesn't happen in Chicago. New Jersey, maybe, but not Chicago.

But there's one thing the denizens of Miami Beach seem to take greater pleasure in showing off than even their children. They love showing off their cars. After all, it's a succinct statement of your disposable income. People just cruise up and down Miami Beach, especially Ocean Drive, showing off their cars and trying to get reactions out of people. Oh, the fleeting glory of being noticed for your car.

Well, my friend Cussy, ever the fashionable fellow, had gone to the trouble of renting a Jaguar S-type for our transportation. That is to say, we had an extremely noticeable form of transportation, perfect for turning the fickle heads of South Florida. Indeed, Cussy took particular glee in pointing out how many more women were checking us out when we got out of said Jag, as opposed to when we were merely walking around, thus forever ending the argument that women really don't at all care about money.

Now normally, I'd put an afternoon of driving around and showing off your car, firmly in the category of masturbatory activities. However, this wasn't an ordinary trip and my travels seldom fall into the category of 'normal."

Cussy, while lamenting how he'd managed to rent the only S-Type in existence without a CD-player, mentioned we should get some manly music, like James Brown. Having an appreciation for the Godfather of Soul, I soon acquired a tape of his 70's Funk Classics. As I put the tape in the Jag, Cussy noted how strange it was to have a pasty-faced white boy and a native of India sitting in a Jaguar, listening to James Brown. That's when we decided it was time to start screwing with people. We decided we should be like everyone else, turn up the bass on our booming speaker system and see how the locals would react to a bit of in-your-face multiculturalism.

Indeed there was a distinct difference in reactions straight down racial lines. The white folks that gazed at the car and recognized the music were unified in their reaction: shock, surprise and disbelief. The black folks pretty much all recognized the music, suffered through an initial double-take and after the double-take, most of them started laughing, having figured out by the volume of the music, that were messing with people. The Latin folks, didn't react at all. Perhaps they're better adjusted.

The best reaction we received came from a black fellow in a green sports car. It was obvious he heard the music and just had to see who was blasting James Brown from a Jag. As he dropped the pedal and pulled his car even with ours and craned his head over to the passenger window to get a look. When he caught a look at Cussy driving, his eyes nearly popped out of his sockets. I glanced over at him and before I had a chance to nod my head, his eyes seemed to pop out a hair further before he snapped his head back and completely dropped the pedal, speeding away from us.

I think we might have violated his perception of cultural rules. Then again, we did that to a lot of people.

There was, however, more fun to be had with the Floridian penchant for automotive excess. Cussy and I had gone to Miami the weekend before Halloween. As a result, we had costumes with us. After attending a costume ball, we decided it was time to put both the costumes and the Jaguar to good use. Cussy was wearing a black cloak and a mask patterned after the film "Eyes Wide Shut," or so he told me. I wore a hazardous materials containment suit, which was alternately called a radiation suit, fireman suit, bomb disposal suit and space suit. Silver foil body, mirrored helmet. You know the drill.

At midnight, all sorts of ne'er-do-wells were cruising up and down Ocean Drive. It took us roughly two hours to make one pass North and one pass South, and the car was probably stopped more than it was moving. The effects were hysterical and straight out of a rerun of Candid Camera. Both of us remained in costume for the drive. I rolled down my window and tried to stick my head out, but the helmet wouldn't fit through the window, so I had to content myself with sticking my arm out. Fortunately, I shelled out for the four-fingered metallic gloves when I bought the costume. I alternated waving, giving the thumbs up and applauding if someone looked like they were getting particularly friendly with their date. On the other side of the car, Cussy just stared at people in the opposite lane of traffic. The results were amusing.

Fortunately, the Miami Beach Police Department liked my costume, or I'd probably be in jail. Really, it was the cops and the senior citizens that seemed to get the most appreciation out of my costume. The cops recognized it and laughed. The senior citizens recognized it and booked out as quickly as their walkers would take them. The rest of the reactions were a mixture of laughter and double takes. Cussy and I had our pictures taken at least a half dozen times, including thirty-seconds of attention from a television camera. We assume we were on the evening news. I had several people come up and shake my hand, including a fellow dressed as the Pope, who assured me "God loves rich people," and gave both Cussy and myself two-dollar bills. We assumed he liked the car.

At various points of this Ocean Drive Odyssey, we cranked a little more James Brown, causing more chaos, as I attempted to dance in the car seat. Soul Brother Number One only added to the confusion, as in costume, you really couldn't tell what race Cussy or myself might be and we got a few more looks for having what was perceived as ethnic music coming out of the Jaguar. Of course, that was more to get their attention, as pretty much everybody got a kick out of the suit.

The moral of the story? It's much easier to mess with people if they have preconceived notions about automobiles and music.

E-Mail From Nigeria

Beset By Hicks:
My Sad Trip To The Alamo Bowl

So Northwestern University, my not-exactly-beloved alma mater, was playing in the Alamo Bowl, in San Antonio, Texas. For those not familiar with Northwestern's football program, there's probably a reason. Counting this one, Northwestern's been to 4 bowl games. The Rose Bowl in the 40's and everything else has been fairly recent. When they had back-to-back bowl years in the mid-90s, I was just out of school and unfamiliar with the concept of vacation funds, there'd been a 50-year gap between bowls before and fearing another 50-year gap (i.e. our star running back turning pro and/or breaking his leg) I figured I'd better make sure I attended Alamo Bowl 2000. As if you didn't know by now, my travels are often a comedy of errors. The error in this trip was trying to attend.

The first thing to do, if you're planning on going to a game is to get tickets. I got screwed, right off the bat. Being a naïve Northwestern alumni, unfamiliar with the workings of bowl games and the high ethical standards of athletic departments, I figure my best shot at non-crap seats was to go through the university. Big mistake. How bad were my seats? 6th row of the end zone. As in, anything past, let's be generous and say past the 20-yard line, allows for little to no perception of depth or distance. If the line of scrimmage is past the 50-yard line, you can only see one team lining up. These seats were so utterly poor, I imagine the only way anyone can sell them is to sucker foolish alumni into sight-unseen ticket applications, much as my dear former athletic department did to me. I suppose if I'd gone to Michigan or some other school that regularly participates in bowl games, I might have known better than to trust the university to provide quality seating. Hopefully if your school goes to a bowl game, you'll make a point of determining their ticket allotment before placing an order.

It could have been worse. After swearing for about 90 minutes, I went to ticketmaster.com and obtained a 35-yardline seat (five rows under the press box). Unfortunately, I couldn't get blocks of tickets by the time I discovered how badly Northwestern had betrayed my trust and since my little sister shouldn't be sitting by herself in a stadium full of Nebraska goons, my parents and my sister, who were already vacationing in San Antonio, got stuck in crap seats. I wouldn't call them cheap seats, as they cost the same as my 35-yard line seat. I don't care what the Alamo Bowl allocated to Northwestern, I'm still of the opinion that if I could get a better seat on ticketmaster.com after enough time had elapsed for the university to process my ticket application and the tickets to arrive through the mail, I've had $160 stolen from me in the form of unusable tickets. (I probably could've gotten a usable block of seats if I'd have gone to ticketmaster.com first.)

I'm supposed to take an early-afternoon flight to San Antonio, the day before the game. When I wake up, it's snowing in Chicago. Since all sorts of flights have been getting cancelled for the previous two weeks, I call the airline. After a couple hours I discover that while my flight is supposed to originate in Philadelphia, the Philadelphia to Chicago leg of the flight has been cancelled, but the Chicago to San Antonio leg of the flight was still on time. Yes, the ticket agent at the airlines headquarters also thought that sounded strange and suggested I call to double-check before I left my apartment. I did and the status hadn't changed, so I headed off to the airport, having no clue whether or not the plane was really there.

E-Mail From Nigeria

It turns out they had to commandeer a flight originating in D.C. and re-route it to San Antonio, instead of the original flight from Philadelphia. As I waited for the plane, I heard Northwestern alums discussing the god-awful tickets they'd received. Well, except for one person who knew their system and had managed to get better tickets than I did. Everyone else was appalled to hear about my face-value ticketmaster.com purchase. Surprisingly, the plane boarded on time, although we did sit on the runway for an hour, de-icing. The funny thing was, we only arrived 20 minutes late. Who says they don't include a fudge-factor in flight times?

After an entirely too long shuttle ride to my hotel, because two freaks wanted to be dropped off at a hotel that wasn't even on my travelers map, it was so far away from downtown, I discovered that not only had my alma mater had screwed me on tickets, but my relatives had screwed me on accommodations. My cousin, who lives in Omaha, not too far from the Nebraska campus, was telling me to register at the River Center Marriott. Imagine my utter joy when I walked into the lobby and discover I'm staying in Nebraksa headquarters. Let me be clear about this. I lived in Nebraska for a short period of time. I'm not overly fond of the team's fans (note that I said fans and not alumni... I have my doubts to how many of their fans actually went there) and quite frankly, Nebraska got screwed pretty hard when an over-rated and lower-ranked Notre Dame team got invited to the Fiesta Bowl instead of the Corn Huskers. These people weren't happy they were in a lesser bowl, and they weren't friendly. Fortunately, I was wearing a black shirt and a black suit coat, not purple, as I didn't want to be reenacting any scenes from "Deliverance."

How sophisticated are Nebraska fans? Well, let me put it this way: I'm wearing a black long-sleeved t-shirt, a black suit coat and a PAIR OF JEANS and they're calling me "GQ." They also seem to think it's an insult. It's probably a good thing I don't wear ties. Well, better dead than red.

All those red sweaters just reminded me of Bobby Knight, anyway, and I hate Bobby Knight.

So after I eat, I go to the hotel concierge and inquire where I should go to enjoy myself. She recommends a martini bar and says I shouldn't bother losing my coat, as the place is a local hang-out and my so-called "GQ" look is normal for the place. So I go to the martini bar and find out just how annoying the Nebraska fans must be. The bouncer at this martini bar is talking to a couple of his friends. He says that none of the regulars are around. He doesn't like this. He says the reason none of the regulars are around is all the Nebraska fans there for the game. He then likens the team's nickname of "Big Red" to a bunch of "Big Red-Necks." I attempted to suppress laughter at a Texan calling a group of people rednecks, although this was a fairly urbane place, even if it was over-run by a bunch of Nebraska twits. (Note: watching Nebraska fans trying to pick up women in a martini bar is amusing... for the first 10 minutes. After ten minutes, you just get depressed.) After the bouncer got done ripping on the Nebraska fans, he asked his buddies if they knew who the other team was. I guess my fellow alums weren't obnoxious enough to get noticed. This same pattern repeated itself everywhere I went the first evening. I learned two things from this evening: 1) I don't like to party with Nebraska football fans; and 2) if the two teams involved are Nebraska and Northwestern, not to expect many women to be around.

How obnoxious were the Nebraska fans acting? Let me put it to you this way... my cabbie told me he'd picked up 2 Nebraska fans at the airport and since it was late and as there weren't many cabs available, he'd convinced them to let a female Northwestern student share the cab with them. The two Big Red-Necks were so abusive to the student (something about her wearing shoes and not being in the kitchen, I imagine), the cabbie almost kicked them out. All the cabbies seemed to be mad at the Nebraska fans.

E-Mail From Nigeria

The next day I met my sports writer, Evil Tony, his Indignant Wife, and his college buddy, The Baron, for lunch. I learned that the Baron's evening flight had been delayed several hours and I was lucky to get out when I did. I also started to notice that the Northwestern people and Nebraska people really weren't mingling very much. Strolling around the Riverwalk, you'd see one table at any given restaurant with a different set of colors than the rest of the tables. For instance, the place where my group ate lunch was a Southwest-style café where even the pizza had beans in it. It was 90% inhabited by people in purple. On the other hand, you quite literally couldn't get within 10 feet of the door of Hooters and it was an overflowing sea of red. I'm thinking these are probably cultural difference between alumni, but to be honest, I really didn't see a lot of places with mixed crowds. Self-segregation? Natural differences? Either way, it was happening.

As I was walking over to meet Evil Tony for lunch, I happened across a trio of young Nebraska fans that horribly offended my mother (not that offending my mother is a difficult task). The oldest of the trio was maybe 16. All three of them wore white paper on their heads, sort of like a cigarette with a big twist at the top. I'd initially thought the children were either trying to be "Red Man Chew roll-your own" or possibly joints, until the "eldest" turned around, revealing the inscription "all I want for Christmas is my first period" in black marker on her faux-tampon hat. You'd think she'd have at least had the sense to write it in red marker. As my conservative, Iowan mother starts to freak out, a white-haired, grandfatherly-looking man in a Northwestern sweatshirt approached the tampon head, told her he had something she should be wearing to go with her sign, and, evil twinkle in his eye, produced a beaver hat. Amazingly, tampon-head seemed to understand exactly what my new favorite alum had called her. My mother however, was even more appalled.

Then there was the actual game. I got to my seat and found that the section had a few scattered Nebraska fans in it, and boy were they morons. The third-dumbest was a fellow in a leather jacket with "Nebraska" down the arm and a pair of biker shorts. I'm not saying the guy looked like a homosexual in the get-up, but the Village People probably would have waived the audition if he wanted to join. He sees a row of people in purple and white ponchos and admonishes them to take off the ponchos, because they should know the game is played inside. He was unable to offer a credible comeback when one of the poncho-wearers pointed out he was wearing a leather jacket, so he must have also thought the game was outside.

The dumbest Nebraska fans, however, had to be the ones about 10 rows in front of me. What kind of an asshole gets arrested at a bowl game? I'm not talking ejected, I'm talking thrown in jail. There were these two unbearable lushes that had nothing better to do than stand up for the entire game and swear at everyone around them for the entire game. And everyone includes a couple small children. They were being enough of a nuisance, one of the local cops had to take them out of the stands and give them a little lecture about shutting up. They didn't listen. Early in the second half, he decided they needed another lecture and Drunken Nebraska Lout #2 decided he was a tough guy. To properly understand how insanely stupid Drunken Nebraska Lout #2 was, you have to understand that he was being a tough guy with 1) a Texas cop, 2)with a gun, 3) that probably weighed in the neighborhood of 270 lbs, 4) and the cop wasn't fat. I asked the cop about what happened. Drunken Nebraska Lout #2 got charged with public intoxication and Drunken Nebraska Lout #1 merely got ejected (and probably spent the evening looking for bail money for #2). The cop was very pissed that he'd had to arrest someone at a bowl game. Like I said, it takes a special kind of moron to get arrested at a bowl game.

E-Mail From Nigeria

The absolute funniest thing at the bowl game had to be the opening ceremony, though. As you may have heard, they like things BIG in Texas. As such, they had an American flag, the size of the football field. They had one person every 5 yards or so holding it, and the side nearest to my seats was running backwards, unrolling it towards the opposite sideline. Well, one of the people unrolling the flag, a rather round blonde woman, didn't have very good balance. She tripped and fell down. Nobody stopped, so this silly woman was under the flag, crawling on her hands and knees, trying to get out from under the flag before anybody else noticed. The flag made it to the sideline before she did.

I don't even want to think about the actual game, with the caveat that while the end-zone seats were truly wretched, the sideline seats were very good. Short lines of sight to the field, though, which means you need to be at least 10 rows up to have a decent view.

When the game was over, I had about 6 hours to kill before heading to the airport. With my luck with planes, and anticipation of not liking the games outcome, I'd booked the first flight out of town in the morning and figured it was early enough, trying to sleep would be dangerous, so I'd forgo the hotel room, find a 4 o'clock bar, then get breakfast and head to the airport.

There was one little problem with that plan. San Antonio is a tame town. They don't have bars open past 2 a.m. Not even on a Saturday night. Spending the last 14-odd years in Chicago and New York, I laugh at San Antonio. These people obviously do not know how to party. To double my misfortune, the game was a late one, and I was busy eating afterwards. By the time my entourage split up, it was 2 am, and I'd had a whole two drinks with my meal, so I was sober with time to kill and nothing open. Well, that's not entirely true. There were three things open. Denny's (fortunately, I'm not currently employed by the Secret Service), something called Sunset Station (which appeared to be having some sort of rap concert, with a much more gangsta crowd than I'd have expected in Texas) and Pollyesther's (a disco/80's dance club whose Chicago branch I avoid like the plague). Of the three, Pollyesther's was the least objectionable. They were open until 4, although their bar was closed. This was one of the few places that a minor mix of Northwestern and Nebraska occurred, largely because it was the only place open. Ugh, what a hopeless crowd. It was also one of the few places I saw some locals. They were considerably less ugly than the bowl people. The best thing about Pollyesther's had to be the Rod Stewart-wannabe. I'm not sure if he was a DJ or the manager. At least he lorded over everything like he was the manager. Other than his hair was a little too short and a little too bleached, he was a ringer for Rod Stewart. The style of dress said it was intentional, too. While I can think of worse people to idolize, I just don't see that many Rod Stewart impersonators. Maybe he's making a comeback?

At 4am, I took a cab to the airport and amazingly, my 6:30am flight left on time. I gather there weren't too many more Chicago flights leaving that day. I honestly can't say if I liked San Antonio or not. Everywhere I went was overrun by the Big Red-Necks. If the locals are complaining about it, who am I to argue? It's just odd I could spend 36 hours in a city and only encounter 5 or 6 of its residents. Chalk one up to unruly guests. I do know the city is way too conservative with the liquor licenses, but at least the Riverwalk staff were nice. Possibly they were just relieved I wasn't wearing red.

Pop Culture

Todd Allen

E-Mail From Nigeria

Something Else To Mix With Your Vodka

Vodka is a very popular mixing drink. You can mix it with just about anything. Coca Cola, orange juice, grenadine, vermouth, cranberry juice, you name it, you can probably mix it.

Going out this weekend, I noticed a group of young ladies switching between two types of vodka drinks: the ever-trendy vodka and Red Bull; and the more traditional vodka and Diet Coke.

Red Bull, being a caffeine-laden energy drink, is useful in shaking off the effects of alcohol, making you feel sober and allowing you to stay out partying longer. We'll just ignore the recent questions about how healthy it is and how many people I've met that compared the feeling of slamming a few vodka-Red Bulls to amphetamines. No, let's concentrate on issue of calories.

Red Bull is an energy drink. As such, it has a lot of carbohydrates in it. Carbohydrates mean calories.

These young ladies had been switching between a diet mixer and a much higher calorie mixer, apparently because they were watching their figures. It's not that some of these ladies shouldn't have been watching their figures. Truthfully, a couple of them were tipping the scales higher than their doctor would recommend, but all diet alternated with Red Bull is little more than posturing, from a practical standpoint. Kinda silly, don't you think? Especially when everybody knows that the lowest calorie alcohol is tequila, not vodka. And if they're typical club kids, they're slamming the Red Bull so they can keep partying longer, that is to say, throw down some more liquid calories.

A pretty vicious cycle for somebody with the pretense of drinking Diet Coke.

Fortunately, I have a solution for all the calorie-conscious vodka lovers out there.

No more need for mixing diet drinks and energy drinks with your booze. You're just denying the inevitable. No, it's time to give it up and order a vodka and Slim Fast. Why bother with a diet drink when your drink can be part of the diet? Why waste the calories eating a full meal before going to the bar, when the bar can be your meal? It's a miracle of modern efficiency, with the added bonus of drinking a liquid meal, you'll probably get ploughed faster and can go home with less alcohol-based calories than ever before.

That's right, vodka and Slim Fast, for when your feeble attempts at losing weight at the bar just aren't silly enough.

E-Mail From Nigeria

The Drowned Out Drummer, Another Insipid Nightclub Fad?

What's up with live drummers at nightclubs? I guess it's the new thing. I slipped into a promotional party when the nightclub show was in town, a few months back, and the centerpiece of the party, other than the booze they were promoting, was a pretty boy drummer. They'd play a tape of some psuedo-techno dance music, and the drummer would play along with the tape, with as many dramatic flourishes as he could work in. It was OK. The main upshot, as I could see, being that the drummer had three or four attractive women huddled around him. Since the rest of the women in the place were, and I'm trying to be tactful here, much nastier than one would expect to find at a nightclub industry show, I can only assume the drummer had his own entourage.

Really, I couldn't say that a live drummer really added that much to the tape, except for giving an air of having live music. Partially live music? Well, it might be more live than some of the lip-syncing darlings of the teen music set, but it's not worth the fuss being made over it.

Not that long ago, I made one of my infrequent visits to a "formal" nightclub. Usually, a couple visits a year will remind me why I don't like Chicago nightclubs. This was no exception. At the far end of the room was the group of people that had summoned me to said nightclub. Toward the front of the room was a DJ booth, and in front of the DJ booth was a set of drums. Yes, this nightclub had a drummer.

What's so unusual about this, you ask? The music from the DJ booth was so loud, I couldn't hear anything the drummer was doing.

Now maybe the DJ and the drummer didn't get along. One owed the other money, so the DJ cranked the speakers to get even. Maybe the drummer just really sucked and needed to be drowned out.

I don't find either theory particularly plausible, as somebody in management was shelling out some cash for the percussionist, and since I was in the room for some 90 minutes, you'd think at some point the manager would have the volumes adjusted to allow his investment to be heard. Didn't happen.

No, I think the club was so pretentious, that they'd heard the live drummers were popular and just hired one to look like they were trendy.   They certainly didn't hire him for the sound. Nobody seemed to be paying particular attention to the drummer, either. Dummy probably should have brought his own posse, but a silent drummer might not be as popular as a loud one. Keith Moon was certainly loud, and not just when he was playing drums.

Of course, this begs the question of whether this particular nightclub feels drummers should be seen and not heard.

I can't say that I've _ever_ met a drummer that didn't want to be heard.

Honestly, I haven't been to enough clubs with live drummers to get a sense for how many of them are actually audible to the crowd. The club I happened into might just be managed by fools hypersensitive to their illusion of styling. Still, next time I go to a place for live music, I think I'll choose one that doesn't involve a stereo.

E-Mail From Nigeria

Oprah To Give United Nations A Spirit Makeover

(New York, NY) – United Nations Secretary General Kofi Annan announced a new program that would have talk show host Oprah Winfrey instructing U.N. ambassadors and workers on making a difference and in self-affirmation, yesterday in press conference at U.N. headquarters.

"For some time, the United Nations has been criticized for moving slowly," Annan told the press. "Being respondent to criticism and believing in the power of change, we looked for philosophical help, both to address public opinion and to bolster any morale that might sag under the weight of such depressing reports of our progress. Initially, we decided on the American philosopher, Franklin Covey, who has a devoted following, and that we would adopt his philosophy of 7 Habits of Highly Effective People."

U.N. sources, speaking on condition of anonymity, confirm that the French objected to adopting an American philosophy to address internal issues and Annan agreed to add a workshop on Positivism, which was developed the Auguste Comte, a French Philosopher and mathematician, in the early 19th century.

"We found that the body of works encompassed by Covey and Comte, while addressing issues of accomplishing goals and of perceptions of reality, did not properly address issues of work satisfaction, pride and well-being," Annan continued. "We were very fortunate that an intern brought the very popular American philosopher, Oprah

Winfrey, to our attention. We observed two of her lectures on television and determined her "spirit-makeover" treatise is exactly what we were looking for. Additionally, we feel that her work in the area of "toxic relationships" will be invaluable to the members of the United Nations Security Council."

Ordinarily, the expense of bringing in a major media star like Oprah might be too much for a financially strapped non-profit organization, such as the U.N. Through negotiations, an unusual bargain was struck. Oprah has agreed to spend two weeks at U.N. Headquarters in New York conducting workshops for U.N. employees and ambassadors, bringing with her some of her regular guests who routinely facilitate such discussions. The workshops will be taped and edited into 4 episodes of "Oprah," for a U.N.-themed week of programming. Additionally, the workshops will be heavily documented and be compiled into a book, which is widely rumored to be earmarked for Oprah's Book of the Month Club. A portion of the profits from the book would be given to the U.N. for use in their general fund. Additionally, Kofi Annan would appear as a guest on a fifth U.N. episode of "Oprah," where he would be given a fashion makeover, as well as discuss the workshops and help pitch the compilation book.

"We have high hopes that this will go far to address concerns about U.N. procedures," concluded Annan. "We look forward to espousing the principles of the great philosophers and hope this will bring us closer to the public at large. On a personal note, I am a looking forward to Oprah re-accessorizing my wardrobe. It is of the utmost importance to appear well-coifed at affairs of state, and such matters are best left to the experts."

E-Mail From Nigeria

Giants At The Movie Theater

I stand 5'10" tall. Depending on where I am, I'm usually considered of average size, or occasionally "big," except, that is, for the last time I went to the movies. There are places for tall people. Basketball and volleyball courts are excellent places for tall people. Movie theaters are not.

The last time I went to a movie, upon sitting down, I noticed that every guy walking into the theater was at least 6'3", and half of them seemed taller than that. Not exactly what you want to find in a theater, as tall guys increase the chance you'll be staring at the back of somebody's head instead of the screen. But it wasn't just the guys that were tall. No, the women with them seemed to all be on the tall side. Not a bunch of six-footers, but plenty from 5'8" to 5'10". I was beginning to feel like there was a sign out side the door that said "you must be this tall to enter," just like on roller coaster at amusement parks, and I was some little kid that snuck in.

As my friend also picked up on our apparent insertion into a re-run of "Land of the Giants," the inevitable happened. Tall people sat in front of us. Actually, it wasn't so much they were extremely tall as the guy in front of me had really big hair. Remember in the 70s when some suburban white kid would think Jimi Hendrix had cool hair and tried to curl his hair into an afro? Yup, I had a refugee from "That 70's Show" sitting in front of me and his ill-kept hair was blocking my view of the screen.

Basically, my friend and I had two options. Either we had to move or we had to make the people in front of us move. Not feeling like sliding over, we started loudly discussing Republican politics and relative merits of George W. Bush. After about 3 minutes, the people in front of us started leaning their heads, paused, then got up and moved. Works every time.

Unfortunately, my new-found bliss at re-discovering what the screen looked like was short-lived. Another couple took the seats in front of us. I knew it was going to trouble when they walked up. Largely because the guy was at least 6'7". They plopped down and we slid over, in an attempt to see more than 1/3 of the screen. Sliding over worked much better, but I noticed that the giants in front of me were leaning in opposite directions from each other, craning their necks at awkward angles. It seemed that there were tall people in front of them, too. Indeed there was a very tall couple two rows up from us, heads so close together, that there wasn't any space between them. You know, the type of closeness that just cries out, "look at us, we've only been getting it on for a week and we can't stop touching each other yet." An annoying enough obstacle, that perhaps it wasn't our offensively political conversation that made the first couple leave their seats. And looking at the "skyline" of heads sticking up from the seats it was pretty obvious what was going down.

Essentially, the taller the person was, the closer to the front of the theater they were, and the net effect was hardly anyone could look straight at the screen without having getting an intimate view of the back of a head. I also think I could have made a killing selling tickets to college basketball coaches and letting them recruit players during the previews of coming attractions.

The movie ended and you might think I left the Land of the Giants. Alas, that's not so. I'd had an economy sized drink and nature was calling (well, screaming might be more accurate). I slid into the bathroom, and there was a giant in the bathroom, too. And it was worse this time. There were three urinals along the wall. Two were being used, one wasn't. Unfortunately, the giant using one of the urinals was so wide (not fat, just a wide frame), that half of his torso was blocking the unused urinal and I had

E-Mail From Nigeria

to wait for another one free up before I could relieve myself.

And when I left the bathroom, I went to bar where I knew I'd be bigger than at least half the clientele.

Todd Allen

Super Models Suppressing Puberty with Performance Enhancing Drugs

(Miami Beach, FL) A breaking scandal on Ocean Drive is threatening to shake the modeling industry apart. Long a meeting point for the international jet set, celebrities and super models, South Beach appears to be a major distribution point for an illegal drug that appears to have gained widespread use on the runway.

Much as steroids have been the performance-enhancing dirty little secret of sports, Polygurg, has taken a similar position for fashion models. While steroids are taken to enhance physical change, generally in the form of added muscles, Polygurg is taken to prevent physical change. Specifically to suppress the changes brought about through puberty.

In an industry where careers start young and a model's career can be over in her early-twenties, it's hardly surprising the drug has found a following.

"I started taking it when I was 16, at the first sign of having hips," Melissa Stickman, now 24, reports. "A fashion designer first introduced me to it, and the waif look has always been favored by the best designers. It's much easier simply not to finish puberty than it is to binge diet."

Indeed, it has been commented that many fashion moguls prefer their wares displayed on a woman with the figure of a pre-pubescent boy, and although the reasons for that preference have never publicly surfaced, it is a reality in that highly competitive job market, and Polygurg is perceived as giving it's user an edge. While Polygurg is incapable of reversing the effects of puberty, it has been shown to suppress natural changes from occurring for up to 11 years.

"The drug works by effecting and controlling hormone levels in the body," Doctor Igor Pedo of the Kinder Modeling Institute, a well-regarded training center in Brussels, explains. "While it does not stop signs of aging, such as wrinkles, it does prevent other changes in the body. While the drug is not legalized in the United States, it is readily available in Europe and Mexico, so its presence should come as a surprise to no one. By suppressing the onset of puberty, it has increased the number of qualified models and prevented age-related lawsuits for many designers, modeling agencies and appreciative politicians."

Not just limited to modeling, Polygurg's use is rumored to have spread to Hollywood, with gossip swirling around several strikingly thin actresses linking them with its use, as well as tales of its abuse by over-the-hill child-stars mistakenly looking for a ticket to past glories.

The major side effect of Polygurg is an intense irritation of the stomach, which can make eating an unpleasant experience for some users. This may actually be responsible for how the drug remained a secret so long, as the side effect is often mistaken for bulimia.

While there has been no official legal reaction at this time, battle lines are being drawn. Fashion insiders are joining forces with such diverse groups as Wonderbra and NAMBLA in an attempt to legalize the drug. On the other side, Weight Watchers, Gloria Steinem and online retailer BiggerBras.com are lobbying to ban the substance.

President Clinton is said to be organizing a federal task force to look into the effects Polygurg has on the modeling industry and, reportedly, will take a personal hand in the interviewing process.

E-Mail From Nigeria

Hannibal Lauded For Positive Portrayal Of Cannibalism

(Washington, D.C.) The activist group, Cannibal Humanization and Anti-defamation in Society and Media (CHASM) publicly praised the film, Hannibal, for its positive portrayal of titular character, Hannibal Lector, as a cannibal.

"More so than other dietary choices, the media consistently casts cannibalism in a negative light," CHASM spokesman Harvey Labinac. "Sure, they were stoning vegans with meat and potatoes in the film, P.C.U., but vegans and vegetarians are not cast as sociopathic misfits with the regularity that cannibals are."

CHASM points to films like "Texas Chainsaw Massacre," "C.H.U.D" (Cannibalistic Humanoid Underground Dwellers), "Ravenous," and "Soylent Green" as examples of media attempts to prejudice the general public against cannibalism.

"What sets Hannibal apart from typical Hollywood fare, is the roundness of the character." Labinac continued. "Hannibal Lector does not live in a sewer. He does not utilize crude woodsman tools for preparing a meal. The Hannibal character is the pinnacle of refinement. The most important thing to Hannibal is proper manners and décor, hardly how the media portrays so-called cannibals like Leatherface. Hannibal takes great care in preparing his meals in gourmet fashion, emphasizing the care it takes to bring out proper flavor in any meal. Dr. Lector is an educated man, spending part of the film working as a historian. Unlike the denizens of C.H.U.D., Hannibal Lector is not only capable of love, but risks his freedom for it. Truly, Anthony Hopkins and director Ridley Scott have done a service to the international cannibal community."

CHASM concedes the Hannibal Lector character to be the only positive portrayal in recent memory.

"The only other thing bordering on a positive portrayal was the musical group, 'The Fine Young Cannibals.' Unfortunately, they were a bit too on the effeminate side to be a truly positive portrayal, and their only popular song, 'She Drives Me Crazy,' emphasized the unfair stereotypes of metal illness among cannibals."

CHASM expressed intentions to create an award to bestow upon Anthony Hopkins.

"The Academy Awards ignored him when he served human flesh in the wonderful film, 'Titus,' and we expect that these recent events and the realistic depiction of his dining will trigger prejudices to keep him from winning an Oscar for this fine work. Between his portrayals of Hannibal Lector and Titus Andronicus, Anthony Hopkins has done more to promote the consumption of human flesh than any other actor of his generation. We our proud that he has given our children someone to look up to."

E-Mail From Nigeria

Just Plain Strange

Todd Allen

E-Mail From Nigeria

The Large Condom Phone Call

I was sitting on the couch, Friday night, watching TV and thinking it was almost time to head out drinking, when the phone rang.

"It's official," came the enthusiastic voice of one of my college buddies.

"Your wife's pregnant," I asked in horror, trying to figure out what he was talking about.

"No, guess again."

Well, I couldn't guess. Which is a good thing, 'cause I'd be one sick puppy if I'd been able to guess the most singular reason my buddy had called.

"Extra-large condoms fit me better," his voice positively beamed over the phone. "I thought you should know."

How are you supposed to react when your buddy calls you up to tell you that normal prophylactics aren't big enough to suit him? Frankly, I was just plain disturbed by the revelation. T.M.I. – Too Much Information. He calls me at nine o'clock at night to tell me this, not during the day, as he is normally wont to do. I'm guessing he'd just found out about his... stature, and felt like bragging. What a jerk!

"You've been married for a year and a half, and you're just now realizing the old condoms didn't fit?" I stammered in state of shock and repulsion, as the sheer depravity of the conversation started to hit me.

Todd Allen

"The normal ones were really tight," my buddy attempted to explain. "It felt like they were cutting off my blood circulation. The large ones fit much better."

Talk about more details than I wanted to hear about.

"So what exactly did you use," I asked, desperately trying to make sense out of the conversation.

"I have no idea," he said. "My wife bought them. I didn't look at the box."

Now you have to understand, my college buddy is a tall guy. He's also inhumanly strong, especially for his fairly wiry frame. Our entire circle of friends has, for 10 years, insinuated that as a tall and inhumanly strong guy, the source of his great power must come from below the belt. And there he is, 10 years later, on my phone, telling me all about it. It's just not right.

I asked him if he'd called our mutual friend, the doctor, as a physician might be better equipped to advise him on the care of his new-found status as a special-needs person. For all I know, he may qualify for some government aid program or anti-discrimination legislation. It also validated the long-standing theory we had on how he could get a "special abilities" green card.

Nope. I was the first phone call he made. If he wasn't married, I'd be very worried, instead of merely repulsed.

It's probably good that I was home when he called. I can't think of anything worse than finding that message on my answering machine, and with luck like mine, I wouldn't have been alone when I played the answering machine. Try explaining that one.

I'm convinced other people don't get this kind of phone call.

E-Mail From Nigeria

The next evening, when I returned from making the rounds, there was another message on the answering machine. It was left around 11:30.

"Magnums," the voice on the answering machine said.

I'm not sure if it's merely his new extra-large brand of choice, or like Tom Selleck's old TV detective, he thinks he's a got a Ferrari.

And I'm convinced, based on the late hour of the message, he was aiming for my answering machine.

Just what you want to hear when you roll in for the evening and are heading straight for your bed: your buddy uses Magnums.

I gotta get caller ID, so I know when not to check the messages.

Todd Allen

... And Then They Stole His Shoes

My friends are notorious for getting me in trouble. This time, one of them almost got me killed with a staggering exercise in poor judgment.

It was maybe 9:30 PM when my friend called me. He'd just gotten off some boat cruise, which hosted a reception attached to a convention he'd been attending, and he needed to meet up and talk with me, pronto.

I suggested a place halfway between where he was and I was, and strolled over. We had our chat, and my friend decided perhaps we should go get his car. I didn't like where he'd parked his car.

The car was parked a couple blocks away from McCormick Convention Center. While that particular neighborhood isn't nearly as bad as it used to be, I didn't think it was any place I ought to be at 11:30 at night, which was the time it was getting to be, and I **knew** it was no place for a suburbanite like my friend to be after dark.

Just to make things even stranger, my friend had been on a boat trip at Navy Pier. For those of you not familiar with downtown Chicago, Navy Pier is a few blocks north of "The Loop," which is downtown Chicago's central business district. McCormick Place is a couple miles south of The Loop, in a... let's be generous here... slightly neglected neighborhood that needs some time to finish the gentrification process. With no traffic, it's probably a good 10 minute drive between the two places, and I've been stuck in rush hour traffic for as long as a half hour trying to get between the two. Suffice it to say, I couldn't figure out why somebody would leave their car at one place and take a bus to the other. Never mind the inherent danger in retrieval, it was just a pain in the ass commuting back to the car.

Not really liking where he'd parked, but figuring he'd probably manage to get himself killed if I didn't tag along, I agreed to ride shotgun on one condition: we would take a cab directly to his car, get in, and immediately leave. (Boy Genius had entertained thoughts of getting a ride the Hyatt by the convention center, and then walking to where he parked the car. While the Hyatt, itself, is safe, I figured leaving it and walking a couple blocks was a lot like holding a neon sign over my head that said "mug me.")

So we got a cab, and I started to have a minor freak out about where he'd parked. 23rd and Cottage Grove was the address. The north end of that particular block ended in a cul-de-sac. There were large construction projects on either side of the street, making it almost impossible to see any traces of civilization from where he parked. I kept thinking of the Lone Ranger, when the Texas Rangers rode into the big canyon with one way out and got ambushed and shot.

Paranoid? Not hardly.

We got out of the cab, and as my friend paid the cabbie, I crossed around to the passenger side.

"You might want to come have a look at this," I told my friend.

The passenger-side window had been smashed in, and the car had been rifled. I wasn't in the least bit surprised, given that the car was left unattended in that neighborhood after dark. Actually, I'd been somewhat relieved the car was actually there at all.

My friend was a little agitated. It took about 30 seconds to figure out they'd popped the trunk and absconded with his laptop. Like I said, it was hard to see any civilized areas from where he parked, so it's not like whoever was breaking in had to be real worried about getting caught, and could take their own sweet time. Or, to paraphrase Orson Welles, these cats would sell no Thunderbird until it was time.

He figured he needed to file a police report for the insurance, so he tried dialing the police, but managed to get cut off, so I told him to sit down, calm down and hand me the phone. Figuring it probably wasn't a great idea to call 911 about a car break-in, I was about half-way through the massive 311 selection menu (it was after-hours, after all, and I was having a little trouble figuring out which district I happened to be in at the time), when I noticed headlights a couple blocks away, heading in our general direction.

At this point, I stopped thinking about the Lone Ranger and starting thinking about "Judgment Night." Judgment Night is a film about some suburban idiots who get lost on the South Side of Chicago and get chased around by gang members.

I was also a little annoyed that we hadn't been there a full 5 minutes and trouble was already coming to look for us.

I told my friend that if the car got any closer, he ought to get ready to start running. I have this nasty allergy to bullets, you see. They make me break out in red liquid and it's quite painful. My friend, of course, was a bit too concerned about his car to have noticed the headlights.

The headlights got closer. Ever notice it's always a 4x4 the people are driving in a situation like this? Really, stereotypes never have a basis. There were two men in the 4x4. One was a white guy who looked like he might have had some Irish blood in him and the other was Hispanic.

E-Mail From Nigeria

They both had the build that said they worked out a lot, but the only exercise they'd ever heard of was a bench press. Ah, the classic gang-banger physique. And they were slowing down at staring at us.

I told my friend to start running if they came to a stop. Fortunately they pulled by us and stopped in the circle at the head of the cul-de-sac, no doubt discussing what weapons to pull on us. My friend decided we should move the car at this point. Fortunately, it started. (Hey, don't laugh, it wouldn't have shocked me if they'd messed with the engine, just because they could, and I was perfectly willing to flee on foot.) The 4x4 was slowing to the halt when we started moving, and then took off. Oh, that famous South Side hospitality. And to think, we didn't have to hang out around Comiskey Park to have an offer to get beat up. These guys were willing to come to us.

We decided it was safer to fill out the police report at police HQ, which wasn't too far. I have to say, Area 1 headquarters has one of the more frightening bathrooms I've been in. Extremely powerful flush on that toilet, too.

It was then that the character of the crime began to shine through. While the car wasn't stolen, the registration had been looked at. Bad thing, that. After all, my friend was from the suburbs. Aurora, the home of Wayne's World. We figure that's the reason they stole his shoes.

Yup. That's right, they left the bills he'd gotten in the mail. They left the diaper in back seat (child's diaper, unused, not one of those adult versions... either my friend isn't kinky enough for adult diapers or the thieves took those and my friend didn't bother mentioning it to the police). They left the jazz CD. Well, actually it was a Van Halen CD in a jazz jewel case. I figure if they'd known if it was Van Halen, they'd have stolen that, too. So these were discriminating thieves... after a fashion.

Still, I have to think they hadn't intended to steal his shoes until they found out he was from the suburbs. You really can't get much lower than stealing a man's shoes. Then again, I never much cared for the suburbs, either.

E-Mail From Nigeria

Porn Bag or Comic Bag?

Mistaken identity is a re-occurring theme in media. On stage, "The Comedy of Errors;" on screen, "North By Northwest;" in print, "The Tailor of Panama." I recently was involved in a case of mistaken identity. Not the identity of a person, but the identity of an object, and it was very nearly as painful as any other case of mistaken identity on record.

The incident started innocently enough. I'd gone to a comic book store to buy my weekly fix of comic books. A young lady I knew came along. She discovered a book on "Tiki Drinks" (you know, Singapore Sling, Mai Tai... Trader Vic's stuff), and thought it was cute enough to buy, so she bought it.

Not too long after that, we ran into her fiancé and a couple of his buddies. They saw me carrying the black plastic bag with my comics in it, snickered, and asked me what I'd been shopping for. I told them "comic books," and produced an issue of Spider-Man from the bag.

The fiancé and his friends looked a little confused and vaguely disappointed.

The young lady then perked up and said, "Look what I bought."

She held up her bag. A look of alarm appeared on the faces of the three men, as her fiancé sat up.

"What did you buy," he asked with a bit of urgency.

She produced the Tiki book and asked him if he thought it was cool?

Todd Allen

The fiancé, clearly disturbed by something, examined the book. "Is this all you bought," he asked, not exactly quietly, glancing suspiciously in my direction.

She said that it was, although there was another Tiki book she wanted to go back to buy, and inquired as to what his problem was.

He motioned to the bags we were carrying. The comic book shop I most often frequent uses plain black plastic bags for its merchandise. The rationale for this is that a number of their customers get embarrassed if people see they've bought comic books, and a black bag conceals the nature of the contents. They've switched bags for brief periods in the past, but customer demand has always made them return to the plain black bags.

Her fiancé was concerned directly because of those bags. It seems, he explained, that these were the exact same type of plain black plastic bags that are commonly used in adult bookstores. I have had a friend or two make an off-handed remark about having a porno bag before, but I'd never really taken it seriously up until this point. In fact, when I'd have occasion to run into her fiancé after buying comics, in the past, he always had seemed vaguely disappointed with the contents of my bag. It also explained a few looks I've gotten carrying those bags.

The contents of my bag were not, however, what was concerning him at that moment. Based on the presence of a shopping bag commonly associated with the adult entertainment industry, he had thought I had taken his woman shopping for pornography, and he was not happy about such a scenario. More unfortunately, he had at least 70 pounds on me, and he was thinking about giving me a beating,

It didn't get far enough for me to go crashing through a wall, basically for two reasons:

E-Mail From Nigeria

1) I didn't take her pornography shopping.

2) She was a lot more upset at the thought of me taking her porn shopping than her fiancé was, and took the opportunity to give her fiancé a small lecture on the subject.

The moral of the story: if you know chicks with large boyfriends, never let them carry black plastic bags.

I'm just glad she hadn't been at Victoria's Secret before we met up. As distinctive as their bags are, I would've gotten hurt before explanations could be offered.

Todd Allen

Plushies – Fetishists Get It On With Stuffed Animals

Ever know an adult who was just a little too attached to their teddy bear? As in like Catherine the Great was a little too attached to her horse? Yup, turns out that sexual attraction to stuffed animals is a bonafide fetish. I probably should be disgusted, but the idea of somebody trying to hit it with a Beanie Baby is just so absurd, I can't stop laughing.

The slang term for people into inanimate paramours is "plushies," although since "plushie" also applies to a class of stuffed animals, the more formal term would be "plushophiles."

For instance, you have "Galen," who maintains a large page devoted to plushies. Amongst his collection of pictures is one of a stuffed animal he finds exciting. This particular stuffed animal is a female rabbit. The good captain expresses great delight that the rabbit's clothes are removable, and posts of series of pictures of said animal in various stages of undresss. (http://velocity.net/~galen/lola.html- I'd call this photo essay much more pathetic in nature, than sexual.)

I admit, when visiting friends' houses, I've been known to rearrange stuffed animals, action figures, and occasionally pets, in compromising positions, but I can't say that I've ever gotten aroused by such activities. Apparently, I didn't spend enough time watching cartoons as a child to develop a truly open mind towards possible conjugal options.

E-Mail From Nigeria

But just posing and stripping stuffed animals, as ridiculous as it may be, is the mildest thing this fetish indulges in. It would seem that some people actually consummate their relationship with plush animals. You wanna read the guide?

http://velocity.net/~galen/psexfaq.html.

Apparently, merely embracing the doll will bring some people to *ahem* gestation, while for others, it's the scent of their little stuffed friend that does the trick. (Since these are plush animals we're talking about, I'm thinking maybe it's related to "new car smell." I've met lots of people that get goofy over the smell of a new car.) There are also the more conventional fans of furry things that make certain... strategic alterations... to their stuffed animals. Apparently the online community has quite the debate going on, as to the best way to clean a stuffed animal. Lynard Skynard used to sing about "That Smell," and it isn't quite the same smell as the soiled objects of a plushie's affections, but I think you get the drift.

The absolute funniest thing about the plushie lifestyle would be the ones that are into "living plushies." That's right. People dressed up like stuffed animals, college mascots, or cartoon characters at amusement parks. If I understand the factors in this fetish, let's just say the San Diego Chicken might be getting a lot more propositions than anyone ever would have suspected.

This stuff is just whacked. And if you peruse a few pages of this type of web content, you'll find a common theme that these plushies find their stuffed animals to be much more trustworthy in a relationship than a sentient partner. Damn! I'm starting to feel extremely well adjusted, what with actually having conversations with real live humans, and all. Then again, I never was a big fan of rug burn, either.

The fellow who tipped me off to the existence of such a bizarre little sect, is fond of saying how the Internet is great way to discover weird things you didn't know existed. I gotta hand it to him: I had no idea such a thing existed, and when I think of a few young women I've known over the years, that still have lots of stuffed animals and are always complaining about what a disappointment their boyfriends are, I just break out laughing. Unfortunately, I don't know any guys with lots of stuffed animals, or believe me, they'd be hearing about it. Right now.

So you want to get a yuck reading about plushies? Better yet, you want to quote a few tidbits to somebody who still sleeps with a teddy bear? Have a couple links that are only PG-13: http://www.velocity.net/~galen/furrydef.html and "Captain Packrat's" www.plushie.info

And to think, I used to find it funny when people merely treated their pets as surrogate spouses. Truly, I lead too sheltered a life.

E-Mail From Nigeria

A Gift Registry For A Birthday Party

It's better to give than to receive, or at least that's the popular adage they use around the holiday season. Some people believe it, others... well let's just say some people don't just believe it's better they should receive gifts, and if you give them half a chance they'll tell you which gift to show up with.

I'm sure you know the type: materialistic young woman moves to the city, gets a boyfriend, gets mad at him, calls him up and tells him exactly which flowers he better hurry up and send over. That's a little forward, but apparently it's only the first step a young woman can take towards the dictation of gifts.

Stop and think about, how often does a person really get the chance to choose what someone gets them? When you're a little kid and you sit on Santa's lap, you're asking for gifts, but you aren't actually telling anyone what to bring, per se. At least, I know an awful lot of people who never got that pony they were demanding of Santa. Occasionally, when you're a little kid, you can dictate what you want if your grandparents are around. That's usually the easiest way to determine your gift. Please take notice; both these examples only work for little kids. Is there ever a time when an adult can dictate their gifts?

Actually, there is one time where you can pretty much get away with telling people what to get you as an adult: your wedding. It's pretty much socially accepted, if not required, that the happy couple get themselves a registry somewhere. I think the original intent was that the happy couple not get a lot of duplicate gifts (I mean, how many champagne flutes does someone need), but if you get right down to it, you're basically telling people what they ought to be getting you for a gift. If you put down toilet paper on your registry, somebody will probably get you toilet paper. That's just how it works. (Don't laugh, one of my cronies DID have toilet paper on his wedding registry.)

Well, one enterprising young lady recently took the concept of a gift registry one step further. She wasn't getting married. No, to the best of anyone's knowledge, she hadn't accepted any proposals. No, she was just having a birthday party. That's right. You were reading correctly. Little Miss Thing had a gift registry for her birthday party.

I can't say I was completely shocked at the development. She always had fancied herself of great social relevance. Still, this was really taking things well into the realm of the surreal. Indeed, I wasn't quite sure if I should take it as a matter of hubris or greed.

Hubris was the first thing to come to mind. After all, registries are usually associated with weddings. And weddings are considered important, life-changing events. Are we to interpret that Little Miss Thing thought her birthday party was as important as a wedding? Registries are there to make sure duplicate gifts don't occur. Did Little Miss Thing think that several people knew her so well that they would all arrive with the exact same item that was the perfect gift for her? Was she also assuming that everyone thought so highly of her that they'd all be bearing gifts? Hey, I've been to a lot of birthday parties where people just showed up with greeting cards and ate some cake. There isn't a damn wrong with that, either.

On the other hand, when you have a gift registry, that's a not-too-subtle way of saying "there's a party and you damn well better show up with a gift." It would be entirely reasonable to assume Little Miss Thing was more interested in the gifts than seeing her friends. Tell you the truth, I wasn't privy to the guest list on this one, so I can't tell you if the circle of invites was widened for optimum gift giving or not. Then there's the small matter of dictating what you want to get, as registries do make a strong statement about one's preference in gifts. The way I'm hearing it, Little Miss Thing had her registry at Pier 1, which isn't exactly a thrift store if you know what I mean. Greed could be motivating factor in the plan.

Be it hubris, greed or a combination of both that drove her quest for material gratification, I got a big laugh out of it. Of course, being a guy, I can't get nearly as catty about the party as the two women who told me about it.

"Can you believe anybody would have the nerve to do something like that," exclaimed disgusted invitee #1.

"I could see it if she had a registry at Borders, so she could pretend she was smart and liked to read," hissed disgusted invitee #2.

I sat back, laughed and took a sip of Guinness, smug in thinking that since Little Miss Thing had sent me a Christmas card and not a party invitation, she must have realized I'd never fall for such a transparent ruse.

Todd Allen

It's All Good – A Slogan For Losers

"It's all good."

How many times have you heard that expression? Some would say it's a philosophy of happiness, acceptance and tranquility. Personally, I think if you're looking for a trite saying to bring you happiness, acceptance and tranquility, you're better off looking for a therapist. "It's all good" is a mantra for losers.

Stop and think about it. How many people saying "it's all good" are actually in a position where everything really is good? Bill Clinton could have been lighting up a cigar, just after finding out he wasn't going to be impeached, said "it's all good," and you know what, in that particular instance, it probably was all good.

But that's not typical of times when that phrase is uttered.

No, more likely, the phrase is uttered under less than ideal circumstances. While at the job and on a particularly unpleasant work detail (say, cleaning the latrine after someone let forth with the Technicolor yawn); in a bar when you realize all the women look like the mythical Bulgarian women's weightlifting team, before they shaved their faces; or when you're eating some particularly badly cooked fast food. Is everything good in these situations? I don't think so.

So what's the proper way to react to a less than perfect situation? Blind acceptance? Revel in mediocrity? Relish being at the bottom of the food chain? That's what you're doing when you say, "it's all good." Oh, the joy of being a defeatist. Nothing like rationalizing depression to get the blood pumping.

Actually, the idea of it all being good, of total equality of experience, sounds suspiciously like a Cold War communist political brochure. "Throw off the yoke of the oppressive ruling class. Proletariat workers united for the common cause. Join a society of equals. It's all good." Yeah, Marxism works so well when applied to real world situations like, say, the continued prosperity of the U.S.S.R. Not.

Sometimes, it really is bad. When Custer rode into Little Big Horn and met up with the Indians, all was not good. When the residents of Palm Beach County Florida couldn't figure out how to use an election ballot, all was not good (for either party). When the Cleveland Browns moved to Baltimore, all was not good.

And sometimes, if the bar you're in isn't all good, you should get up off your ass and go next door. I guess "it's all good" doesn't account for wanting to better your situation in life.

The thing that just kills me about this insipid little phrase is the total lack of ambition it supports. If it's all good, is there any reason to have ambition? Why work hard for a promotion when you can just collect on your unemployment insurance? After all, it's all good. No need to have pride in yourself. You don't need to prove anything in a world where it's all good. It's a wonderful smooth transition to joining the cult of low self-esteem.

Teddy Roosevelt had this philosophy called "rugged individualism," wherein a person could take responsibility for their lives and make something of themselves. If you weren't at the top of the heap, that you, given the opportunity, should be able to elevate yourself above the quagmire around you. He called this raising yourself by bootstraps, or "bootstrapping." If somebody told Teddy

Roosevelt that it was all good, Teddy would probably whack them with that big stick he was always talking about carrying around.

No, "it's all good" is a refuge for the losers in life. People content in their misery.

So next time I'm walking by Morton's Steakhouse, holding a bag of carry-out from MacGreasy's fast food, and some under-dressed twit with a girlfriend the size of an oil tanker and a complexion to match, tells me it's all good, don't be surprised if I give him a boot to the head. By his logic, lying in the gutter should be just as good a place to be as anywhere else, and I just might want to eat some steak next week.

E-Mail From Nigeria

Beggars On The Bridge

When there's a lot of road construction going on, things tend to change. You have road detours, you have dust being kicked up, but this time I've found something more bizarre happening. Chicago, as you may or may not know, is tearing down and totally rebuilding Wacker Drive, one of the main roads in the downtown business district called "The Loop." As the construction moves, some of the bridges get shut down for a few days, which has created a sort of real estate shortage. Why would you call it a real estate shortage? Because ever since the construction has begun, the Wabash Street bridge has been overrun by bums and beggars jockeying for position.

Prior to the construction, one of the two sides of the bridge would normally have a destitute asking for a handout. About half the time, both sides will have someone panhandling. Now, however, the real estate shortage is making people double up. Two, sometimes three beggars on one side of the bridge.

I'm not talking about Streetwise dealers (homeless who sell a special charity-newspaper, instead of pan-handling, although it really amounts to a sort of license to beg, as most people aren't buying the paper for it's content), who tend to be more polite and bathe more frequently. I'm talking sitting your run of the mill, sitting on the ground with a cup, looking for change beggars. Their societal function, according to sociologists who pontificate on such subjects is to make you feel good when you give them money, as it reinforces that your life doesn't suck in comparison.

As the situation has played out, it's been interesting to watch the patterns. Used to be, there were a couple different beggars that staked out the bridge and held court in roughly the same spot on a regular basis. Squatter's rights you might call it. Then you started having two beggars on one side of the bridge... unless the guy in the wheelchair showed up, in which case, he'd usually be the only guy on that side of the bridge. I'm guessing the wheelchair got enough more sympathy that the other beggars were losing money to him and conceded one side of the bridge to that guy. I suppose the hand-out business has unfair competition, just like any other business.

Well after a while, you'd start to see three beggars on one side of the bridge, or maybe just two, with the third one lying on the ground next to the entrance to the bridge. Yeah, that's an appetizing site when you're on your way to get lunch. Oh, wait, a lot of the pan-handling business, and it can be a business, is about applying guilt (which of course, allows you to feel better for yourself after you've been shaken down for some coin), not unlike some of these ads for child development programs that prey on guilty parents who feel they don't spend enough time with their kids.

After a couple days of three bums to a side, the turf wars started. Well, that might be over-stating it a bit, but seeing as how the beggars haven't unionized or anything, you start to see them get in arguments over who really ought to be begging where. This can be a very interesting site to see, especially if they're screaming at each other and trying to panhandle at the same time. People generally try and get out of the way when a couple of bums are having a violent argument. This is what a real estate shortage does: makes prime locations more valuable and up the stakes. I'd love to see the look on the face of whoever planned the project, if said person was asked to comment on the Wacker construction project causing turf wars among beggars.

I'm figuring the reason this Wabash bridge gets more beggars than the Michigan Avenue bridge, which generally just has one beggar one each side of the bridge, and even then, they're usually of the street musician variety, which is less annoying, and even amusing on occasion, is that there aren't many tourists on the Wabash bridge. No, it's preferable to let the working stiff get panhandled, rather than exposing the tourist.

They seem to have opened up a couple more bridges to foot traffic in the last week, and I haven't seen any more three beggars to a side days. Then again, I did see one of the regular beggars, switching spots and trying her hand at selling StreetWise, which would, theoretically, be a step up in the world. On the other hand, she wasn't wearing shoes, while selling StreetWise, so I'm not entirely sure what to make of it. Still, her departure might have freed up some space for bums lower on the food chain.

Me, I'm waiting for them to enact a law that limits beggar capacity on bridges, just like the fire marshal has maximum capacity for theaters and restaurants. If its an absurd situation, you might as well have an absurd solution.

Todd Allen

Suburbanites Don't Know Drums

It never fails to astonish me how stupid people can be. Especially the suburbanites. Is there some sort of law stating you cannot have a clue if you live in the suburbs? Sometimes I wonder...

On the Sunday before Labor Day, I was summoned to the neighborhood adjacent to Wrigley Field, home of the Chicago Cubs, to attend a barbeque. Unfortunately, the Cubs finished their game surprisingly quickly, and instead of arriving during the seventh-inning stretch, the game had already let out, and the stadium was freshly emptied. That is to say, getting off the train, I was walking into a big mess.

A sane man tries to avoid Wrigley Field as a game is about to start or has just ended. The sidewalks are overflowing, you can't walk anywhere without essentially being in a line, and, more often than not, everyone is bombed.

I hadn't been by Wrigley after a weekend game before. I didn't notice any drunks, but I did notice the suburbanites. Easy to spot, they were. The nuclear family: mommy, daddy, and two very young children that probably aren't old enough to actually understand they're at a ballgame, but are old enough to walk, or should I say, wander around and make mommy chase after them. Naturally, being from the suburbs, they were a paler shade of white than even my own pasty self. The nuclear family was everywhere, and they weren't moving. No, they were standing around, staring, and making it impossible to get around the stadium. I don't mind people staring at things, as long as they're not staring at something silly. Needless to say I was about to be annoyed, because they were clogging up the sidewalk too much for me to move.

E-Mail From Nigeria

The silly little suburbanites were fascinated by street musicians. Now it's OK to be fascinated by street musicians, as long as they're GOOD musicians. I'm frequently fascinated by street musicians in New Orleans. I'm infrequently so moved by street musicians in Chicago. There are two or three of note, but I was especially not moved by the street musicians in question.

The suburbanites were staring at gaping at drummers. When wandering downtown, most often in front of the Wrigley Building (as opposed to Wrigley Field), you might run into some decent drummers. They play complicated rhythms and riffs. They play bongos, or sometimes just drum on large plastic pails, like you might find paint in.

The drummers at Wrigley Field were drumming on plastic pails. They were young children. I'd guess the age of most of them at about 12 years old. They were paired up in groups of two or three, and I ran into two sets of them as I tried to walk past the stadium. There could have been more. These children were all drumming the same cadence. It was not complicated rhythm they played. In fact, it was nothing more than a basic marching band cadence. The type you learn in junior high, if you're in a marching band. Or at least it's the basic cadence they teach you if you're in junior high in Iowa, as I was, some time ago. This is not remotely sophisticated stuff.

I have to wonder why the suburbanites were so fascinated. It certainly can't be because they love marching bands. Nobody pays that much attention to a marching band. Was it because the children were drumming on pails? It's not like that's an unusual thing in the city. Was it because the children drumming on the pails were black, and they don't have many black children in suburbs? Trust me, if the suburbanites were from the North Shore, this is possible. Did they think, because the children drumming on the pails were ethnic, that they were playing some special ethnic folk music? I imagine that's what it was, more than anything else.

Todd Allen

Sorry suburbanites, you were dropping quarters into the cups of some kids that were just playing something they were taught in school. Funny that you'd give them more money if they were in street clothes banging on a pail, than you would if they were in a band uniform and marching. Heck, it's also a whole lot more difficult to play the drums when you're moving, than it is when you're sitting down. What a bunch of clueless twits. If I thought the children were performing an activity closer to free enterprise than begging, I might think differently, but it had the look and feel of begging. Kind of like the blind accordion grinder and his monkey, arguing with Peter Sellers in "The Return of the Pink Panther."

You almost feel sorry for the suburbanites. Such a lack of musical sophistication.

You just don't see this sort of thing at Comiskey Park, where the White Sox play. Oh, I'm sorry, White Sox fans tend to be more urban than suburban, many of them being of an ethnicity other than caucasian.

The real question is, what mundane activity can I do to convince the suburbanites to give me money, too?

E-Mail From Nigeria

Understanding What The Policeman Says

I just don't understand why people have so much trouble with the police. Cops really aren't that hard to get along with. I think it's all in understanding exactly what they're saying. For instance, if a cop says to you, "do you want to go to jail," it means he isn't going to arrest you, unless you starting mouthing off to him, that is. If he wants to arrest you, he'll be too busy slapping the cuffs on you to ask about your preferences. Alas, most people aren't smart enough to realize what the police are really saying to them, and proceed to mouth off.

Last weekend I had the opportunity to hear some more of the special language of the police. This happened when the party I was at got raided. First time I've been at a raided party since I was at college. I've had building management knock on my door, but no armed interlopers. There's a first time for everything, I guess.

So I'm on a rooftop in a relatively fashionable section of the Chicago Near North area. The hosts decide to crank some tunes. This lasted for somewhere between 5 and 10 minutes. After a song, there was some debate over how loud it should be cranked and the music was shut off as it was discussed. As this discussing was starting to take place, we noticed the police had shown up. Given that the police were there within 15 minutes of music being played at 9:00 PM on a Saturday night, you have to figure my friends must have some real freaks for neighbors.

As there wasn't any music when they got there, the cops looked around and seemed to decide they had more important things to do, like investigate shootings, but one of the neighbors wouldn't let them leave. Yes, one of the neighbors dragged them out of their car twice, because he just couldn't stand the idea of music being played on a Saturday night. Did I mention the neighbor in question was an art critic? Figures, don't it?

So eventually, the police make it up to the rooftop. One of them comes on to the roof to look around, the other one stays in the stairwell. I suspect this was because he was just too large to step through the doorway. The guy really should have been on the Bears' defensive line. He definitely would've started for the Vikings.

Cop number one realizes there isn't anything illegal going on, and explains to the host that they've had two shootings in their district and they needed to get back to that. He further told the host the standard, in the police manual, line about inviting neighbors to parties, and said that he really didn't want to come back, and if he did, he would have to ask people to leave the roof.

Now if you know cops, that really wasn't a big deal. That's even lower on the threatening scale than asking somebody if they "want to go to jail." What the cop really did, in the form of issuing a warning was to say, "Look, I've got some shootings I need to deal with and your neighbor is a real freak. If you make more noise, not only is that time I can't spend dealing with real crimes, but I'd have to talk to your neighbor again. I really don't want to get nagged by him again, so could you pleeeeaaaaaase keep it down?"

And the funny thing is, the art critics of the world actually think the police are dedicated to stamping out loud music before 10 PM, as a priority. (Never mind that 11PM is the official hour that outdoor venues are closed for noise reasons, or the jack hammers from the city construction in my neighborhood that never started before midnight.) And I'm sure his sheltered little mind never detected the distaste that the constables had for his incessant whining.

E-Mail From Nigeria

If only more people understood exactly what the police mean when they say things, we have many less misunderstandings. And maybe the cranks would find a different venue to express their dissatisfaction with life.

Todd Allen

Fluffy Toilet Seat Covers

There are some things men are probably not genetically coded to understand. The unyielding need for multiple pairs of shoes, what's so special about Keanu Reeves... and fluffy toilet seat covers.

Fluffy toilet seat covers? That's right, those overly plush covers that slip on top of the lid of the toilet. They can be a plain, solid color, they could be a pattern (perhaps a flag), a holiday theme (a Santa Claus for Christmas or a pumpkin for Halloween), or even a face. They're also bloody annoying.

There are two things that really bother me about these covers. The first thing is a question of necessity. Why do you need the things in the first place?

Think about it. Most public restrooms don't even have lids in the first place. You've got the toilet seat and the toilet bowl, that's it. The only reason to have a lid is to keep small children and/or your pets out of the toilet. Will your pet appreciate seeing Santa Claus on top of the toilet? I doubt it. Will your small child? Quite possibly, in which case your child will probably be more likely to play with the toilet, which I gather is not the desired response.

Beyond the practicality of said toilet lid, is the whether or not the lid is even used. Does anyone really sit on a toilet with the lid down? Granted, people are supposed to sit on a toilet seat, but to sit on the closed lid? No, that's not a common occurrence, nor do the lids appear to be constructed to support a great deal of weight. Thus, I'm even more incredulous as to the value of a plush, carpet-like covering for something nobody is going to be sitting on in the first place, let alone care how soft it is.

So are we left with the idea that porcelain is unattractive and should be hidden? Is the color white out of fashion in the Fall and Winter months for bathrooms, as well as for formal society functions? The notion just seems silly to me.

The second problem I have with them is a bit more severe. Women and men differ in their toilet habits. Men commonly utilize the toilet from two positions, whereas women generally only use one. (For purposes of brevity, I am counting sitting and hovering over a public toilet as the same position, sorry ladies.)

Normally, men are the only ones that use the toilet from an upright position. I say normally, because I'm not sure how to count RuPaul, and I've heard a few stories about women going upright on a dare or bet. But normally, the upright position is the province of the Y chromosome.

As a man who has the occasion to use the toilet while standing, I have encountered a design flaw with the fluffy toilet seat cover. A cover sufficiently fluffy to appease the average interior decorator is thick enough to cause problems. Often, and this has happened to me in a variety of locations, the thickness of the fluffy cover prevents the seat from attaining a 90 angle to the bowl. This can cause gravity to affect the seat, and pull it down to its original sitting position.

From the female perspective, this is not an entirely bad idea. Many women complain that men leave the seat up. Certainly, if gravity pulls the seat down, milady need not worry about plopping down and missing the seat. Alas, gravity was not created with a built in time delay. It tends to pull the seat down after only a couple seconds. Just enough time for a fellow to start his business, if he's not paying attention to the surroundings. If a fellow isn't careful, the falling motion of the toilet seat can cause a big mess.

So ladies, I ask you, implore you... for the sake of any unsuspecting men that should wander into your lavatory, dispense with that fluffy toilet seat cover. Neither of you want to make a mess.

E-Mail From Nigeria

The Migratory Effects Of The Smoking Ban

So it's been a few weeks and we're starting to get a taste of dear Mayor Bloomberg's ban on smoking in bars. People seem to have good luck connecting with members of the opposite sex while taking a puff on the sidewalk outside of bars. (We'll reserve formal judgment on that tactic until it's been tested in a January snowstorm.) The bartenders I've spoken to don't seem incredibly concerned about any weekend business drop-off, just yet, although one keeper of the tap did find a drop-off in weeknight business. Time will tell us how this plays out.

My greatest discovery of the new era has been the odor of the men's room at one of my local haunts. Good lord! Without the smoke covering the almost tangible scent, my initial reaction was to retreat to the hallway. I've since toughened into it, and I'm sure they'll eventually get a couple pine trees in there.

As a non-smoker witnessing all this, I'm not always personally affected by the law, and while I don't mind a lack of haze, I'm still thinking its legislative overkill. Quitting of your own free will is preferable to legal enforcement. Perhaps Attorney General Ashcroft could lend his opinion on a smoker's civil rights? After all, rumor has it Mayor Bloomberg is looking to expand his smoking bans. We've all heard stories that Central Park is the next place for smoking to be banned. That may not be the second stop on the anti-smoking trail, after all. The way I hear it, the next stop will be a ban on smoking in the bath tub, which is apparently fraught with danger not only to the smoker, but to any plumber that may happen to be fixing the sink.

And while the public seems to be counting the impact in terms of business patronage, it is at least as important to track another emerging trend: anti-smoking legislation's effect on the migratory pattern of celebrities. Oh, you scoff, but already political pundit, author and mini-skirt aficionado Ann Coulter has already announced her move to Miami out of disgust over the smoking ban. And really, when somebody who leans as far right as Coulter does starts referring to anything as fascist (her view on Bloomberg's "smoking police), I start paying attention.

But as one bird migrates south, will not another take her place? Without smoke, the tobacco user is lead to other forms of the substance. Without a pipe or cigar, that leaves a decidedly less erudite form known in its user's vernacular as "dip" or "chaw." That's right; I'm talking about that traditional favorite of baseball players, chewing tobacco. What's more American than baseball? I'm sure 'ole Bloomy is just being patriotic while narrowing tobacco usage to "a pinch between your cheek and gums." It must be a bid for the All-Star game.

One wonders, does John Rocker "dip," and if so, will the Big Apple's de facto endorsement of chewing lead him to overcoming his misgivings towards our fair city? We have Ann's celebrity void to fill, after all.

Will there be a city tax on spittoons?

Will New Yorkers protest the long-standing, but, dare we say, illiberally named brand, "Red Man Chew?"

For that matter, what will be done to curb the flow of Nigerian scam e-mails offering to smuggle exotic Cuban chaw into Manhattan, circumventing the city tax, yet never delivering. Will the victims feel safe to report the crime? And you thought Bloomberg was mad about those Indian reservation smokes. Wait 'til our favorite offshore conmen get done with the city.

Oh, what will the future bring? We conclude this exercise in reactionary political satire with the quandary: if you

E-Mail From Nigeria

can't smoke in your bath tub, can you chew in it, and if so, can you spit far enough not to sully your water?

Todd Allen